# HISTORY UNDER FIRE

*By the Same Author*

# LONDON FABRIC
## By JAMES POPE-HENNESSY

*With a Colour Frontispiece and over 50 Illustrations from Paintings, Prints and Photographs*

*Demy 8vo*                    10s. 6d. net.

❧

". . . A sensitive, informative, and remarkably skilful book . . . deserves the most vehement recommendation."

RAYMOND MORTIMER
in *The Listener.*

" He displays, not merely a sensitive taste in books and pictures, but a fresh and original literary gift . . . in its delicacy of touch and veiled humour the book reminds me of one of Paul Morand's early masterpieces."

HAROLD NICOLSON
in *The Daily Telegraph.*

". . . deserves a place on the most fastidious Londoner's bookshelf. There is an edge in the observation, a distinction of phrase . . . and much London lore handled with care."

*The Manchester Guardian.*

AWARDED THE HAWTHORNDEN PRIZE

❧

Published by
B. T. BATSFORD LTD.
15 NORTH AUDLEY STREET, LONDON, W.1

*The Western Campanili of St. Paul's Cathedral,
seen through a Victorian shop-front*

# HISTORY UNDER FIRE

52 Photographs of Air Raid Damage
to London Buildings, 1940-41

by

CECIL BEATON

With a Commentary by

JAMES POPE-HENNESSY

LONDON
B. T. BATSFORD LTD.
15 North Audley Street, Mayfair, W.1

MADE AND PRINTED IN GREAT BRITAIN
FOR THE PUBLISHERS, B. T. BATSFORD LTD., LONDON
TEXT BY THE DARIEN PRESS, EDINBURGH
PLATES BY JARROLD & SONS LTD., NORWICH

# PREFACE

THIS illustrated commentary on some aspects of the London air-raid damage deals with a deplorable by-product of indiscriminate bombing—the destruction of irreplaceable buildings, whose beauty and historical associations have made them famous. In providing the text for Mr Cecil Beaton's splendid photographs of the ruins I have tried to avoid both abuse of the enemy, and sentimentality over the wreckage. There was no need for such emphasis, since the photographs are explicit and tell their own tale. Two comments, however, may be made here. In the first place it is patent that the bombing of buildings, however ancient and magnificent, cannot be considered as criminal as the bombing of living civilians. In the second place we should admit that certain English buildings, by their proximity to military objectives, must inevitably be destroyed. The London docks, like those of Hamburg, are legitimate objectives ; St Paul's Cathedral is not. I have termed the destruction of historic buildings a by-product of indiscriminate bombing, because we cannot sanely suppose (or ask others to do so) that enemy bombers single out any specific church or company hall to attack. On the other hand, I feel that we are safe in assuming that the destruction of Allhallows Barking, of Hogarth's villa, of several rooms in Kensington Palace, of Wren's St Lawrence Jewry, does not inspire the Nazis with remorse. Their attitude to the history and the public monuments of Poland and some other of the countries they have conquered shows an inflexible determination to erase the dignified and treasured memorials of a national past. We are, then, not surprised to find our historic buildings attacked. We are only surprised that the damage has been less widespread than two years ago we should have feared.

There is no adjective to describe the spasm of disgust that we experienced, last September, at coming suddenly upon the gaping shell of some London church, or the crazy house-fronts of a placid Georgian crescent that had been bombed. It was a sensation that those who have not lived in a bombarded city will never understand ; but in so far as it is possible to convey the early horror of the ruins, and also their melancholy appearance, Mr Beaton's photographs do this. In taking them he has earned the gratitude not merely of contemporaries anxious to assess the damage to London history, but of posterity ; for surely his series of ruined churches, streets and houses may prove as documentarily important as Hollar's engravings of the area devastated by the Great Fire of London in 1666. The merits these photographs display in other ways—composition, grandeur, tragedy, the strange vitality of wreckage—are too unusual and too evident to require indication.

Though the subject of this commentary is one calculated to arouse the anger of every Londoner, the plan and purpose of the text may be less clear. When at the very beginning of the air raids on London in September 1940, the Gothic hall of the Merchant Taylors Company, and the Gothic church of the Austin Friars were bombed, we were shocked though not astonished. It had happened at last. Our own medieval buildings were being reduced to the dusty rubble with which we first became familiarised through newsreels of the Spanish Civil War. Since September 1940 a good many London buildings of all dates have been damaged or totally destroyed. While realising the extent of these losses, have most of us any precise conception of what some of these buildings have represented in the past ? I do not know how many people visited the Merchant Taylors Hall each year. Very few, I suspect. We have a tendency to mourn the disappearance of places that we have never seen, or of which we know nothing. It is with the aim of preserving a few of the associations of bombed buildings that I have chosen pieces of information relevant to them, bracketed these loosely into periods, and presented them as a running commentary upon Mr Beaton's photographs. The commentary is in no sense whatever a comprehensive record of London damage. That is a task for experts. My intention has been merely to suggest something of what we have lost in London during the winter of 1940 to

1941. I am certain that the quality of the photographs should raise this little book above the level of a pure tract for the times. By the date of its publication we may well have lost more beautiful and more important buildings than those tabulated in the present volume. But I do not see that any extension of the bomb damage in London, any further casualties amongst Georgian terraces or City churches, need make this short statement of the results of a winter of destruction either ephemeral or out of date.

J. P.-H.

# CONTENTS

Page

PREFACE . . . . . . . . v

I. THE ATTACK ON MEDIEVAL AND RENAISSANCE
LONDON . . . . . . . . 3

II. THE ATTACK ON WREN'S LONDON . . . 42

III. THE ATTACK ON HANOVERIAN LONDON . . 93

INDEX . . . . . . . . 115

The Fire-fighters of London—
under George I and George VI

*Chaos by St. Paul's: looking from Ave Maria Lane
across the site of Paternoster Row*

# HISTORY UNDER FIRE

I

## THE ATTACK ON MEDIEVAL AND RENAISSANCE LONDON

*Modern Bombing and the Great Fire—Four London Churches—
Ruins of the Austin Friars—Lay-out of Medieval London – Old
St Paul's—Ruins of Allhallows Barking—Trial of the Templars
at Allhallows—Burials from Tower Hill—Executions on the
Hill—Lady Jane Grey at Guildhall—Duchess of Gloucester at
Guildhall—Ruins of Guildhall—Ruins of St Giles, Cripplegate
—Milton's Statue—Frobisher, Foxe, and Stow—Church of St
Andrew Undershaft damaged—Broken Windows in St Olave's—
Charterhouse saved by Fire-fighters—Damage in the Temple—
Tombs in the Round Church—Ruins of Middle Temple Hall—
" Twelfth Night " produced—Lambeth Palace damaged—West-
minster Hall—Coronation of Henry IV—Westminster Abbey—
Funeral of Henry V—Sandbagged Tombs in the Abbey—Burial
of Neville Chamberlain.*

AN attractive but ill-considered parallel has lately been
drawn between the damage done to London by German
bombs and the destruction of the city in the Great Fire
of 1666. It is a wholly false comparison. Bombs demolish one
precious building, or set a small section of the city alight: the
Fire of 1666 burned London medievalism to ashes in five days.
It was the funeral pyre of the Middle Ages. The real tragedy
of the air-raid damage to medieval London lies in the fact that
we had anyway so little of medieval London left. Churches
which had survived the Dissolution of the Monasteries, the
Fire of London, and the onslaught of nineteenth-century
development are now being bombed.

Until the close of 1940 there were four medieval churches

of primary importance in London.   Ignoring Westminster Abbey (a monastic foundation away over the water-meadows, far outside the city wall) and regretting old St Paul's (burned in 1666), you still had four tremendous examples of medieval London church building : the Austin Friars, St Bartholomew the Great, Allhallows Barking, and St Helen, Bishopsgate. These four churches used to seem four corner-stones for any imaginative reconstruction of the Plantagenet city.   In 1940 two of them were wiped out in air raids : the Austin Friars blown to bits by high explosive, the church of Allhallows-by-the-Tower burned to the ground.   So far St Helen (originally the church of a large nunnery, and filled with alabaster tombs), and St Bartholomew, the most spectacular Norman structure in London, are unharmed.

The Austin Friars is one of the very worst individual instances of bomb damage within the city.   It was a light Gothic church: it is now a rubbish heap.   Unlike the ruins of Wren churches burned in December 1940, the Austin Friars or Dutch Church is simply unrecognisable.   Except for the traces of three Gothic arches outlined upon the east wall, no one would guess what sort of a building stood here.   The Austin Friars is not a picturesque ruin : its slender pillars and great fourteenth-century windows, its elegant Gothic arcades, were not strong enough to stand up to high explosive, and there is now nothing upon its site but pieces of stone, lengths of sodden planking, smashed tiles, red telephone books hurled from a nearby office by the bomb blast, a mound of curled lead (as elaborate as Richard II drapery), and a stack of iron railings.

The Augustine Friars house in Old Broad Street Ward, founded in the reign of Henry III by Henry de Bohun, was one of a series of big London monasteries.   In our day it was the only portion of one of these to remain.   The thirteenth century was a time of active piety : we find the Earl of Kent setting up a Dominican House in 1221, the Carmelites or White Friars building a monastery and church twenty years later, the Franciscans or Greyfriars establishing themselves at much the same moment, the Crutched Friars with their monastic house at the corner of Hart Street.   These great foundations were some of the first to fall during the period of sixteenth-century destruction we call the Dissolution of the Monasteries. Victims of that pack of wolverines, the Tudor rich, they were gutted and torn down, and their stones used to construct palaces for the new nobility. The Austin Friars Church provided an excellent example of this process. It was granted by Henry VIII to Sir William Paulet, the venal old courtier who became Marquess of Winchester: when asked in Queen Elizabeth's reign how he, who had been born in that of Richard III, had come so prosperously through the political turmoils of the whole sixteenth century, he candidly answered, " By being a willow and not an oak." Paulet converted the monastic buildings of the friars into his town residence, Winchester House. The church itself, a very large Gothic building, had been reserved by the Crown and was given by Edward VI to foreign refugees from religious persecution on the continent. It remained in their hands till its final demolition in 1940 as the Dutch Church. The young king's grant did nothing, however, to deter the Paulet family. For centuries the Austin Friars had been a burial place for the great: among over eighty personages of consequence buried in the church, Stow listed the barons killed at Barnet Field, the Earl of Surrey beheaded in 1397, the Earl of Oxford beheaded in 1461, the Duke of Buckingham beheaded by Henry VIII. The spacious transepts were blocked with monuments worth many thousands of pounds: all these Lord Winchester's son sold for a hundred pounds, and with them the lead stripped from the roof. He made stabling for his horses in another part of the building. This behaviour, quite characteristic of the vulgar Henrican aristocracy, shocked Stow and all Londoners: but worse infamy was to come. The Mayor and Corporation of the city petitioned Lord Winchester to have the steeple of the Austin Friars repaired. The fall of the steeple, they pointed out, would bring " a great deformity " upon the whole city, for it was one of the sights of London ; its present condition was, too, a public danger. Lord Winchester replied to the petition by ordering the steeple to be pulled down, and with it the choir and the transepts. The foreign refugees and the proud citizens were left with the empty nave. It was this nave, with its vacant Sandraert atmosphere, that one knew as the Dutch Church. It was a dignified and roomy church, and though the absence of transepts, choir, and funeral monuments was disheartening, there was a passivity about the Dutch Church that Westminster Abbey with its jostling generations on their brackets and their pedestals can never achieve. It was a placid authentic piece of medieval London, and though in this century it had been dwarfed by tall adjacent office buildings till it seemed a diminutive chapel crouching behind iron railings, the Austin Friars is an irreplaceable loss. Even should the Dutch rebuild this church, as they have said they will, its worn beauty cannot be re-created ; for it was an achievement of the slow and sliding English centuries.

The Great Fire of 1666 is largely responsible for our present ignorance of medieval London. To grasp the lay-out of the old city is not, however, an impossibility if we consider its component parts. Firstly, there was London Wall. Secondly, there was the River Thames. Then there was the Tower, the Cheap thoroughfare, and the colossal cathedral of St Paul. The rest of the city consisted of houses and shops of wood, of the stone palaces of bishops and the great nobility, of priories, colleges, hospitals, and big stone churches. Round about the city lay pasture land, orchards with unpollarded trees, detached farms. Down the river was Greenwich, and the Palace of Placentia : upstream across the fields Westminster clustered round the Abbey, the Palace, and the Great Hall. Elsewhere lay scattered villages like Whitechapel and Islington, and recreation grounds like the Moor Fields, with butts for archery practice. London Wall was high and impressive. It had turrets all along it, and large gates at Aldgate, Bishopsgate, Cripplegate, Aldersgate, Newgate, Ludgate, and Bridgegate. Bridgegate gave access to that peculiar feature of the city, London Bridge, with its nineteen stone arches and double row of houses. Built at the end of the twelfth century, London Bridge was as a matter of fact always falling down. The piers required constant mending : in the central pier was the crypt of the chapel of St Thomas à Becket, where daily mass was celebrated just above the level of the Thames. " Shooting London Bridge " was for generations a dangerous but dashing performance; it almost drowned the Duke of Norfolk in 1428, and two centuries later gave Henrietta

6

The Austin Friars,
or Dutch Church,
to-day

e Austin Friars:
m a 19th-century
drawing

*All Hallows, Barking to-day and in the 19th century*

Maria a miscarriage. Barges and water-traffic would be sent rushing down between the piers, and often the boats would be smashed or overturned by being thrown against one of them. The Tower of London, high on Tower Hill, guarded the approach to the city from the sea. It had many uses: a fortress, a royal living house, a prison, a minting place, an armoury, and a treasury. Westwards towards Ludgate Hill stood the smaller towers of Montfichet and Baynard's Castle. But the building which truly dominated London minds was the Cathedral of St Paul.

Old St Paul's was in silhouette rather like Salisbury Cathedral, though it was longer and its spire was taller. At its west end rose twin towers, in one of which, the Lollard's tower, the bishop's prisoners were immured. The cathedral was supported by flying buttresses, those architectural insects' legs. At the east end was a great rose window, through which the light seeped quietly, casting a smooth uniform glow upon the pillars of the nave, the chantries and chapels, the monuments that thronged the transepts. The tombs of St Paul's were as splendid, perhaps, as those of Tewkesbury: John of Gaunt and Blanche of Lancaster side by side beneath a crocketed canopy, Henry de Lacy on his table tomb, his hands joined in prayer, the memorial of Bishop Roger Niger, the brasses of Braybrooke and Ralph de Hengham—these were but a few. Later the Elizabethan monuments overshadowed those of the Middle Ages: and these in their turn were overshadowed by the ostentatious marvel erected to commemorate Sir Christopher Hatton. It was this showy tomb that elicited a Jacobean epigram:

> Three years together in this town hath been,
> Yet my Lord Chancellor's tomb he hath not seen.

After the fire of 1666 only one bishop remained intact of all this funerary world: a charred group of figures from the tombs is to-day lodged at the east end of the crypt of Wren's cathedral: the rest, with their canopies, shields, pinnacles, lions, and mitres, were pounded up to make mortar for the new building.

Like its city, St Paul's has always been in danger from

9

outbreaks of fire. Rebuilt in 1251 (two years before the foundation of the Austin Friars) of Caen stone after its destruction
by fire, the body of the cathedral stood unaltered till 1666.
The steeple, however, burnt once in 1087, was attacked by
flames in 1544 and 1561. After this last conflagration, caused
by lightning (people on the river affirmed that they had seen a
spear-shaped flame strike at the spire from the thunder clouds),
the spire was not put up again. Its loss was badly felt, and the
fire caused some consternation :

> For five long hours the fire did burn,
> The roof and timbers strong,
> The bells fell down and we must mourn,
> The wind it was so strong.
> It made the fire,
> To blaze the higher
> And do the church still greater wrong.

St Paul's spire meant a great deal to Londoners: on festival
days, the coronation of Mary Tudor, for example, someone
would mount the steeple and wave a tiny flag in joy. Beneath
the cathedral was the crypt called St Faith under St Paul's,
and another little church stood not far from the big west doors.
In the churchyard was a bell tower with four Jesus bells ; this
tower was said to have been staked on a throw of the dice by
Henry VIII, who thus lost it to Sir Miles Dugdale. In one
of the cathedral cloisters was the famous frescoed Dance of
Death. On this *macabre* but realist note we may now leave
our consideration of the lost cathedral church.

The Fire of London, which burned the fabric of old St
Paul's ("the stones of Paul's flew like grenadoes," Pepys tells
us) and so many other churches, spared that of Allhallows
Barking, on Tower Hill. It swept up Tower Street "on both
sides with infinite fury" and was checked at the church porch.
But the church had been badly injured in an explosion in 1649.
A new brick tower had to be built : ironically enough it is this
squat Cromwellian addition that has best withstood the modern
fire. Allhallows Barking, the most complete medieval church
in all London, was burned out on that December night of 1940
which saw the disappearance of the Guildhall and of eight Wren

[Planet News

*The City, December 30th, 1940. Wren's Cathedral*
*ringed by fire, but saved: a contrast to the burning*
*of St. Paul's in September, 1666, shown on the next page*

*The Fire of London, September, 1666:*
*from an engraving in Wilkinson's "Londina Illustrata"*

*The City, night of December 30th,* 1940

churches. More is left of Allhallows than of the Austin Friars, but it is precious little. The fourteenth-century east wall has collapsed, revealing a gaunt toppling warehouse, with sooty windows: in the churchyard a few trees raise Japanese branches at the sky: and through the traceried window frames along the south wall we gaze down at a small street of desolation below.

The date of the first foundation on the site of Allhallows is not known. The name of Barking is thought to come from the Abbey of Barking in Essex: the name was already in use in the twelfth century. Undoubtedly a Norman church occupied the site of the Gothic Allhallows: but the church London generations had come to love consisted of thirteenth and fifteenth century masonry. Apart from the 1649 damage and the subsequent restorations, Allhallows had come down to us comparatively unscathed: its scorched ruins are heartrending. So far we have been thinking of medieval London in terms of stone and pillars, of tombs and monuments. With the aid of two inventories of the fittings of Allhallows we may imagine this church as it would have appeared to a sixteenth-century parishioner—I say sixteenth century because the Henry VIII inventory is far more thorough and more businesslike than the other drawn up in 1452, when Henry VI was on and off the throne. We could, if we cared, go into the church with the Reformation Commissioners, those hard-faced men who sized up the material value of the piety of earlier generations. The interior of this big Gothic church is dim: light filters stiffly through the stained-glass windows (those same windows that now give on to wreckage and a burned churchyard). Before the rood glimmers an oil lamp: other lamps twinkle at the side altars and the chantry chapels. Let us make it early morning, with priests in red vestments murmuring the mass, and candles in their latten and silver candlesticks shining clearly on the clasps of the missals. Upon the rood the silver-plated crucifix flashes as it reflects these spots of light. The altar frontals are red and white: at the little side altars (and in the sacristy cupboards) are frontals of blue sewn with gold roses, of green and red with golden flowers, a white one with apostles' heads upon it. At each side of the small altars hang curtains held by jutting ironwork rails: green curtains painted with angels and white

15

roses, for example, or like the choir curtains, deep blue. The black frontal for dead masses at St Nicholas' altar is of worsted, with the crucifix, the Virgin Mary and St John figured upon it; for the side curtains of this set are hangings of black sarsenet. Inside the sacristy we may see the censers of gilded copper or silver, the silver one made from a girdle bequeathed to All-hallows by a pious parishioner. But what is happening to these fifteenth-century stuffs and metals? To the placid priests? To the lamps and the candles? To the very arcades and the window frames? It seems a church of a different date, an earlier date. And who are these inquisitors? These two bishops? This trial that is to our eyes like the Shaw trial of Joan of Arc? It is the trial, in Allhallows in 1311, of the English Grand Master of the Knights Templars.

In 1308 the new King of England, Edward II, that foolish monarch whose serene beauty we admire upon his Gloucester tomb, was persuaded to follow the example of King Philip of France and arrest the Knights Templars. The knights, for two centuries a major power in European politics, belonged to an order taking its name from its Jerusalem stronghold, a portion of King Baldwin's palace upon the site of the Temple of Solomon. They were one of three great military orders founded in the twelfth century. Their specific objects—the protection of roads to the Holy Land, the defence of pilgrims and the conversion of the irreligious—involved a certain exemption from episcopal jurisdiction. Implicit in this exemption lay possible Church hostility: the wealth and power of the Templars, especially after the fall of Acre had deprived them of their nominal *raison d'être*, caused considerable jealousy. Philip of France, who saw that their property was well worth seizing, was easily convinced that they were guilty of every crime and sin; denial of Christ, spitting on the Cross, greed, homosexuality, and pride. After some disagreement between King Philip and the Pope (and a conference on that romanesque hill-top, Poitiers) the order was suppressed in France. In Paris the knights were put to torture to extract confessions, and when the arrest of the English members of the order failed to produce much evidence against them, Edward II ordered torture to be applied to them in the Tower. In April 1311 the formal examination of the Grand Master and some other of the knights opened. It was held in Allhallows Church.

The Templars had at first settled in Holborn when they reached London in the twelfth century: in 1184 they moved down to the river, near Fleet Street. After the seizure of their property, the round church and the buildings attached to it were given to the Knights of St John of Jerusalem, who leased the Inner and the Middle Temple to students of law. Brought before the Papal Inquisitors and the Bishops of London and Chichester in Allhallows Church, the Grand Master and his companions carried themselves with dignity and wisdom. The result was a reapplication of torture. The courteous denials of guilt continued. At length some sort of an agreement was reached: and the members of the suppressed order were told to recant publicly, and that they would then be publicly pardoned, in St Paul's. Five of the knights, too old and ailing to get to the cathedral, were dragged at sunrise to the church of Allhallows, to recant there in the chapel of St Mary. This chapel, which stood in the churchyard, had been founded by Richard Cœur de Lion. The Lion's heart itself was at one moment thought to be buried beneath St Mary's altar: but it has been concluded that it lies in Rouen, as originally intended. The chapel of St Mary was made a royal chantry by Edward IV. This act of royal piety did not save it at the Dissolution, and the chantry was suppressed in 1547 and pulled down in 1548. For some time the site was left vacant: but in Elizabeth's reign Sir William Winter, a merchant, erected a warehouse for his sea-borne goods upon the ground.

The situation of Allhallows churchyard made it a normal burial place for the headless blood-drenched bodies off the scaffold on Tower Hill. Bishop Fisher's emaciated corpse was brought out of the Tower to the churchyard in June 1535, and tossed naked into a trench dug by some soldiers with their halberds because they could not find spades. Surrey the poet was interred here in 1547 before being trundled down to his elaborate tomb at Framlingham in Suffolk. Much later Archbishop Laud (whose nephew Layfield had a chequered career as Rector of Allhallows) was buried in the church until the removal of his body at the Restoration of the Stuarts to

17

St John's College Chapel, Oxford. Under the Tudors executions on the Hill came to form an even more integral part of every-day London life than in earlier reigns. Stow tells us of the huge timber scaffold waiting ready for prisoners handed over to the London sheriffs to be put to death. Tower Hill (an open space to the north-west of the fortress, with houses and gardens on it) was the scene of countless executions : here and at Smith-field (where people were burned, boiled, and hanged) and Tyburn Tree (or Deadly Never Green, near what is now Con-naught Square and Marble Arch) people were constantly being killed on charges of treason or heresy or murder. We are correct to think of Henry VIII's reign as outstanding for the number of its executions. By sanctioning the decapitation of two of his own wives, queens of England, King Henry had unconsciously demonstrated that no immunity lay in eminence, no safety in intimacy. There was a danger about sixteenth-century London life as great as that of the Wars of the Roses in the fifteenth century, or of the Cavalier and Roundhead wars of the seventeenth. But it was a different danger. Sudden death no longer came in battle only. At Flodden, Musselburgh, or Guinegate, death was conventional and authentic; but executions like those of Queen Anne Boleyn, Queen Catherine Howard, Thomas More, Lady Shrewsbury, or Lady Rochford were unlike the political murders of previous centuries : they were novel, and they made everyone distinctly apprehensive. As we look at the Tudor courtiers whose faces and characters—those tight-lipped cautious faces, those pliant characters—Holbein has preserved for us, it is hard to realise that every one of them was living perilously. At any moment one amongst them, with the customary angular clothes, the customary Renaissance jewellery, the customary preoccupation with wills and houses and land and wealth, the customary obedience in religious and material matters, might perish on a wooden scaffold. To regret such a victim publicly was to run a grave risk oneself. And enough of them did perish : Fisher and More in 1535 : old wrinkled Lady Shrewsbury, the mother of Cardinal Pole, was beheaded (after running wildly round the block) in 1541 : Thomas Cromwell, with his new earldom of Essex, his Italianate mind, his wiles that had failed, and his

*The Banqueting Room,*
*Guildhall, and* (below)
*the Nelson Monument*

*St. Giles' Cripplegate:*
*clearing up after the first bombing*

little pig eyes, in the same year: Surrey the nostalgic poet:
Lord Seymour of Sudeley, executed by order of his brother the
Protector: then two years later the Protector himself: and
then Sir Thomas Wyatt, the Duke of Northumberland, Lord
Guildford Dudley, the Duke of Suffolk, Lady Jane Grey:
these were but a few of the notable personages killed within or
without the Tower precincts in the middle of that century,
beneath the cloudy London sky we know to-day. At the name
of Lady Jane Grey one instinctively pauses, wondering about
that wraith of English history the nine days' queen, and thinking of that poignant inscription IANE IANE upon the wall of the
Beauchamp Tower, said to have been cut by Guildford Dudley
himself. Lady Jane Grey was always, one feels, in conflict
with her environment: she would never have fitted into the
Tudor age; her death seems quite natural and preordained. We
cannot connect her properly with the crude intrigue that
brought her to the throne, the vulgar battling of her ennobled
relations trying to snatch at the English crown. Erudite and
retiring, she had no more desire to be Queen of England than
she had any legal right to that position. Yet once she had been
established (the first woman ruler since the Empress Maud)
and had begun to sign documents in her tough, decorated hand-
writing " Jane the Quene," she showed a quite unexpected
wisdom and obstinacy. When Lord Winchester brought her
the crown to see whether it would fit, she at first refused to
put it on her head, for she knew it should not fit. When
Winchester casually added that another one would be made
for her husband, she said firmly that she had no intention of
making him king: she would give him no title greater than
that of Duke. Her stand upon this point was the occasion of
a number of angry wrangles between herself and Guildford
Dudley. Shut up in the Tower she became so frightened that
she ordered the keys of the gates to be brought at night to her
own apartments. Besides the Crown of England they brought
her a jewel casket from the Jewel House: it contained the
ornaments of previous kings and queens; gold buttons, a gold
toothpick like a fish, tablets studded with sapphires and other
stones, a silver newt, some small agates, some turquoise beads,
a pair of bracelets of flame-coloured amethysts. Some of these

jewels, perhaps, had belonged to Queen Anne Boleyn or to Queen Catherine Howard.

If one thinks of Jane Grey in the Tower (a portion of which has been injured in air raids) one thinks of her still more as one wanders through the ruins of the Guildhall. She was brought here to be tried in November 1553 with her husband and her brothers-in-law. Ranged before the accused was an impressive show of Tudor authority : the Lord Mayor, the Lord Chancellor, the Duke of Norfolk, the Duke of Suffolk, and many members of Queen Mary's Council. Lady Jane stood before them, a Charlotte Brontë heroine, a mild girl of seventeen with a pretty, heart-shaped face, brown squirrel eyes, a smooth pale forehead : she wore a black French hood, and was dressed in a gown of black cloth, with a black cape lined with velvet. At her girdle hung a little book with a black velvet cover, and she held another book in her hand. It was in these clothes that she was beheaded in the following February.

The Guildhall, burned in 1666 and again in 1940, was often the setting for important trials. Culpepper and Dereham, the virile lovers of poor Catherine Howard, had been sentenced to death here in the 1540's, and it was at the Guildhall that Eleanor Cobham, Duchess of Gloucester, had stood before her judges in 1441. The Duchess of Gloucester, who was thought to be under the spell of the Witch of Eye (burned at Smithfield in the same year), was accused of sorcery and necromancy, and suspected of treasonably trying to get the crown for her own child. The assembled bishops in the Guildhall condemned her to do public penance for three days : carrying a taper in her hand, she walked on the first day from Temple Bar to St Paul's, on the second from the Swan in Thames Street to Christchurch, and on the third from Queenhithe all the way to St Michael in Cornhill. The remainder of her life was spent in confinement. In spite of these and many earlier historical associations, the wreckage of the Guildhall is the wreckage of an ugly and synthetic building. The blackened rafters lie heaped under walls, staircases, and arches of Romantic Revival Gothic ; here and there are patches of the medieval structure, pieces of the shell of the fifteenth-century Guildhall that have survived two fires. The colossal marble groups, monuments to Wellington and Nelson, Lord Mayor Beckford, and the two Pitts, have come through the fire fairly well. But it is not of these pieces of sculpture (neither more nor less interesting than many similar specimens within the Abbey or in the aisles of St Paul's) that we need think in the Guildhall, and if we must picture city banquets let it be the peacock feasts of the Middle Ages rather than those of modern aldermen or the Restoration orgies Pepys and other diarists describe. The Guildhall of the city already existed in the twelfth century, though the building in which Jane Grey was tried was not erected till the year 1411. From a little cottage (runs a *naïf* and much-quoted account of the Guildhall) it became a large and fair house, and under the will of the pantomime mayor, Dick Whittington, the hall was paved with Purbeck slabs and its windows glazed with representations of the Whittington arms. Public-spirited citizens weighed in with more money for more Purbeck and more glazing, and one of them gave tapestry for the mayor's throne. This great central hall was perhaps like a smaller edition of Westminster Hall, with arches, pillars, and arcades, and Edward the Confessor's arms on shells up in the spandrels. The real beauty of the Guildhall, however, lay in its entrance porch. This porch, partly burned in the Great Fire, and reconstructed in the eighteenth century by Dance, had seven statues in its niches. These figures are listed in a Tudor ballad :

> Where Jesu Christ aloft doth stand,
> Law and Learning on either hand ;
> Discipline in the Devil's neck
> And hard by her are three direct,
> There Justice, Fortitude, and Temperance stand ;
> Where find ye the like in all this land ?

The old Guildhall was burned on Tuesday, 4th September 1666 : " That night," we are told, " the sight of Guildhall was a fearful spectacle, which stood . . . for several hours together, after the fire had taken it, without flames . . . in a bright shining coal, as if it had been a palace of gold or a great build-ing of burnished brass." The Guildhall we knew, constructed upon the calcined fragments of the fifteenth-century walls, was an example of later generations' misconceptions of the Gothic world.  Its fresh destruction is an historical rather than an artistic loss.

Whittington, who left money for the paving of the Guildhall, was a benefactor to the city in other ways as well.  His executors used his money to make improvements to the water supply: arching over a pool of water near the vicarage of St Giles, Cripplegate, and building stone steps down to the spring.  They also restored a " bosse " of clear water in the wall of St Giles' churchyard.  The church of St Giles, Cripplegate, a late Perpendicular building, damaged by fire in 1545 and famous as the burial place of Milton, has now been destroyed in an air raid.  It was never a very exciting church, and it is chiefly for its associations that we must regret its demolition.  Dying in November of 1674 John Milton was laid in the same grave as his father, at the upper end of the chancel in St Giles, upon the right-hand side.  The hackneyed story of how his remains were disturbed in 1790, and his teeth sold by the verger to the curious, is probably baseless.  Many people thought the body dug up at this time was that of a young girl and not of an old poet, though the whole incident called forth many protests, including Cowper's verses :

> Ill fare the hands that heaved the stones
> Where Milton's ashes lay,
> That trembled not to grasp his bones,
> And steal his dust away.

St Giles has suffered on several occasions from bombing : on one of them the modern statue of Milton was blown clean off its pedestal and lay upon its back on the ground for some days.

The fire of 1545 (when England was again at war with France, and Frenchmen had landed and camped in the Isle of Wight) did enormous harm to the church : Wriothesley the Windsor Herald reports in his chronicle for that year that nothing but the walls were left, and Stow notes that few of the monuments escaped the flames.  In the reconstructed church three outstanding Tudor characters were buried.  They were Sir Martin Frobisher the navigator, John Foxe the martyrologist, and John Speed, historian and cartographer, who made coloured maps of the English counties for the members of

*Milton's Statue blown from its pedestal outside*
*St. Giles' Cripplegate. In this Church the Poet*
*worshipped and was buried*

*The Lion and the Unicorn
from Wren's pew in St.
Margaret Pattens*

*Monument to John Stow (1525?–1605): erected by his widow,
Church of St. Andrew Undershaft*

Archbishop Parker's Society of Antiquaries. Frobisher, who died in 1594 of a wound received during an expedition to relieve Brest, was one of the most enterprising and the loneliest of Elizabethan explorers. His full-length portrait hangs in the Bodleian Library at Oxford : a tall, bearded man, whose life had been spent voyaging to Guinea, and in an icy search for the North-west Passage, in expeditions to Meta Incognita and Jackman's Sound, to the Countess of Warwick's Island and Frobisher Bay, and, too, a warmer and more exotic experiment in the emerald waters of the hot Caribbean Sea.

Few English books of the sixteenth century are more satisfying to handle than the volumes of Foxe's *Book of Martyrs*. With their narrow double columns of black-letter text, thick and uncompromising, their lively German woodcuts of burning heretics and haughty popes, these folios have a special vitality. The matter of the *Book of Martyrs*, bald but laborious anti-Roman propaganda, has all the charm and vigour of sincerity : it only lacks the additional merit of being true. The *Book of Martyrs* was first printed in 1563, after its author's return from a voluntary Calvinist exile in Frankfurt and in Basel. He had gone there in 1554, when his appointment as tutor to the children of the dead Surrey had been taken from him at the accession of a Catholic queen : he had been chosen for the job by the children's aunt, the widowed Duchess of Richmond, the pallid daughter-in-law of Henry VIII. Profoundly Protestant, Foxe spent the rest of his life much as we might expect : preaching at Paul's Cross, opposing when a Canon of Salisbury the repair of the cathedral fabric, disseminating the austere heresies of the Genevan reformers. His activities ended only with his death, and the body of the hardened old Protestant was at last laid to rest in the church of St Giles.

Far more memorable, and also far more neglected, than Foxe is the great sixteenth-century chronicler John Stow. Stow has been generally recognised as the most painstaking and accurate historian of his age : he himself said that he wrote neither from fear, favour, nor malice, but only for love of the truth : in this he was the antithesis of Foxe. Originally a tailor, he began about 1560 to form a collection of manuscripts; and from producing scholarly editions of Chaucer, Matthew

27

Paris, Matthew of Westminster, and Holinshed, he came to writing a *History of England* and a *Survey of London* himself. His *Survey* is often referred to in these pages : it is indeed to John Stow's amazing curiosity and careful energy that we owe the complete account we have of Tudor London.  It is thus especially disheartening to find that his monument in St Andrew Undershaft (a tall, cold, and rather vacant medieval structure with a fine roof that has been damaged in the air raids), is wholly unprotected.  The monument shows Stow seated at his table, writing : in his hand a feather pen, renewed each April by the Lord Mayor.  He is very grave and quiet sitting there in his tippet and his ruff, with his eyes cast down upon the book in which he writes.  Ben Jonson used to refer to him as a " merry old man," and his executor has left a description of Stow's appearance :  tall, lean-faced, with small bright eyes and a cheerful expression, with a good memory to the day of his death and admirable sight ;  sober, mild, and courteous to anyone who came to ask his advice.  The church in which he still perilously sits writing, oblivious of the overhead danger, derives its strange name of Undershaft from a maypole or shaft put up outside it every year.  This maypole, taller than the church steeple, was last raised on the evil May Day of 1517, when the prentices rioted and attacked foreigners.  The pole was laid along the exterior of the church wall on iron hooks, until a preacher in the reign of Edward VI called it an idol and egged the crowd on to cut it to pieces.  Stow, " an admirer of antiquity in religion as well as in history," and suspected of being a recusant, was much disgusted at this needless vandalism. Throughout his *Survey* he records Henry VIII's dissolutions and seizures of Church property with marked if restrained distaste.

As slightly damaged as St Andrew Undershaft, is Pepys' Parish Church, St Olave, Hart Street, which escaped in the Fire of 1666.  St Olave's has now lost some of its windows. The destruction of so much Victorian stained glass in the city churches is a happy by-product of the bombings : never, one trusts, will parishioners again be able to commission the kind of coloured windows which have for decades disfigured St Mildred, Bread Street, and other churches.  A narrower escape than that of St Olave's is the survival of the Charterhouse, that

28

piece of Oxford in London, founded by Sir Walter Manny, of whose heroic exploits Froissart's chronicle is full. But it is not with Manny but with the Howards (and most particularly with Foxe's pupil and patron, the hasty Duke of Norfolk, beheaded in 1574) that one links the Charterhouse. Like the Paulets at the Austin Friars, the Howards made the Charterhouse buildings into a town residence, constructing the grand airy staircase which gives access to their chain of state-rooms on the first floor. The balustrading of this staircase is of dark wood, that carved plum-pudding woodwork so characteristically English, so essentially Elizabethan. The Charterhouse, low-arched, full of tiny quadrangles and courts, and with one of the most gorgeous of all Elizabethan tombs in its chapel, was saved owing to the efficiency of its fire-fighting service.

Before going down the river to Lambeth Palace and the damaged interiors of Henry VII's Chapel and Westminster Hall, we must pause at what used to be Temple Bar and look for a moment within the Temple precincts. Here the damage is considerable: the peaceful brick-lined courtyards, with plane trees and flagstones, are filled with rubble: some of the sedate houses where generations of lawyers have had their rooms have been eviscerated:

> Those bricky towers,
> The which on Thames broad aged back to ride,
> Where now the studious lawyers have their bowers
> There whylome wont the Templar Knights to bide,
> Till they decayed through pride.

Even Spenser is not immune from the bombs. Once inside the Temple it is irresistible to enter the circular Temple Church, built by the Knights Templars whose trial we observed in Allhallows, and dedicated by the Patriarch of Jerusalem in 1185. This church, one of the four left in England on the plan of the Church of the Holy Sepulchre (with a rotunda attached to the west end of the nave), was liberally restored in the nineteenth century; but it contains some of the most precious and the most lovely tomb-figures in the country: the recumbent effigies of thirteenth-century knights, made of dark polished freestone, lying in two groups upon the floor of the round church. These effigies once rested properly on table tombs : but cleaned and painted in 1706 and (far more menacing) "conscientiously restored" just one hundred years ago, they were not permitted to stay where they were meant to be. And so they lie, black and sculptural, at one's feet. How can one describe the appearance of these knights ? The attitude of each of them is different : some have their legs crossed, some have them straight : the heads of all but one are supported by a cushion : three have helmets, one a monk's cowl, one a great casque : some have a lion or a dragon at their feet, and a great sword by their side. A few of them have been identified : Robert de Ros, Baron Ros of Helmsley in Yorkshire, who died early in the thirteenth century, has a bare head and flowing hair. The three successive Earls of Pembroke of the Marshall family lie together : powerful nobles of the courts of Richard I and Henry III, they now recline stilly on the Temple floor. These two groups of Templar Knights, with their contorted legs and swirling jupons beneath their chain-mail tunics, are quite unlike the stiff inanimate effigy of Rahere in St Bartholomew's ; they have all the frozen beauty of eternally suspended motion, and the smooth sure elegance of birds : they seem to float upon the pavement of the Temple, beneath the early Gothic arches, like a flock of black swans.

Some of the windows of the Temple Church are blown out, and the outside walls are scarred and shaken. Far more widespread, and more generally regretted, have been the great injuries done to the Middle Temple Hall. This Hall, where for centuries the students of the Middle Temple ate at long oaken tables and drank from pots of green earthenware, was constructed in 1572. One hundred feet long, it was one of the finest examples of an Elizabethan hall in England : it had a great hammer-beam roof with pendants, and a famous high Renaissance screen, wrongly supposed to have been made from the spoils of the Armada. This screen has fallen down, though its decorations are not entirely destroyed. But apart from the beauty of the Hall, and the traditions it enshrined (the " old but riotous " custom of feasting which Evelyn deplored, the appearances of royalty at entertainments, Henrietta Maria coming there in 1635, " putting off majesty " and in a citizen's

*The Middle Temple, and
one of the Templar Knights
from the Round Church*

*Scene of the first recorded performance of "Twelfth Night," February, 1601–2: The Middle Temple Hall*

*Débris from the shattered screen*

habit), the Hall was of international importance as the scene of the production, in February 1601, of Shakespeare's *Twelfth Night*. John Manningham, a student of the Temple, noted in his diary under this date: "At our feast we had a play called *Twelve Night* or *What You Will*. Much like the *Comedy of Errors* or *Menechmi in Plautus*, but most like or near to that in Italian called *Inganni*." How well one can fancy that first playing of *Twelfth Night*: the end of the hall lighted by torches and candles, the gold-thread clothes and the trim spangles of the actors, the hollow music of viols from the minstrels' gallery, the intricate shadows cast by the carvings of the screen. Outside in the Temple Courts it is a blowing winter's night, the trees tossing in the wind and the lonely Templar Knights immutable upon their table tombs in the little round church. An attuned but drunken audience is watching this early incarnation of those deathless creatures Olivia, Orsino, Viola in her boy's clothes, Malvolio in his yellow garters, Maria, Aguecheek, and Sir Toby Belch. Outside the great Hall (which glows like a huge lantern in the night) it is London in February: inside it is a mythical city and an imaginary sea coast:

> Vio. : What country, friends, is this ?
> Capt. : This is Illyria, lady.
> Vio. : And what should I do in Illyria ?
>   My brother he is in Elysium.

It is, too, Olivia's garden, where that mournful fantastical widow utters her doting cynicisms :

> How shall I feast him ?   What bestow on him ?
> For youth is bought more oft than begged or borrowed.

And then, while the minstrels in their gallery pluck at the taut strings of their instruments, we hear those songs which, with their dulcet and unanswerable hedonism, have become the property of all the world :

> What is love ? 'tis not hereafter ;
> Present mirth hath present laughter ;
>   What's to come is still unsure :
> In delay there lies no plenty ;
> Then come kiss me, sweet and twenty,
>   Youth's a stuff will not endure.

Who would not give his life to have been, for that single evening, callow John Manningham ?

Less universally significant, but almost equally incongruous in its own way, was the persistent bombing of the Archbishop of Canterbury's Palace upon the river at Lambeth. This great house (it came to be called Lambeth Palace at the beginning of the nineteenth century : as we might expect) lies close to the Thames, so close indeed that for centuries boatmen plying up and down used to doff their hats to the image of St Thomas à Becket that stood in a niche upon the Lollard's Tower. This stone tower was built by Archbishop Chichele (the founder of All Souls at Oxford, who died in 1443), and its upper room is lined with very thick wood panelling, with iron rings in it, and names cut by a knife : evidence that made people assume it to have been an early prison, and to call it, unsuitably, the Lollard's Tower. It may have been in this tower that the Earls cf Essex and Southampton spent the first night of their arrest after the rebellion against Queen Elizabeth in 1601 : it was thought better to keep them at Lambeth till morning, because of the danger (which we noticed earlier in another context) of shooting London Bridge at high tide and in the dark. At the very highest tide, as a matter of fact, the gates, walks, and cloisters of Lambeth House would be quite flooded ; and Archbishop Laud, who kept a careful, curious diary, has recorded the discomfort this used to cause him. When Laud was brought to trial in 1644, one of the earliest accusations the Commons called on him to answer was why he had set up popish images in the glass windows of his chapel at Lambeth. "Amongst others," it was stated, " the picture of Christ hanging on the Cross " and " of God the Father in the form of a little old man, with a glory, striking Miriam with leprosy." Prynne told the elderly prelate that it was obvious he had had these pictures copied from a " massbook." Laud answered by explaining that the chapel had been in such a state of disrepair that " I was ashamed to behold, and could not resort unto it but with some disdain, which caused me to repair it to my great cost." The window pictures were not copied from any mass book : he had had them put together from fragments which he had found there, and which he had

" compared with the story." But refutation could not save that consecrated head.

Beneath the Lambeth Chapel (an Early English building with lancet windows and a modern roof) is a crypt. This is the oldest portion of the whole palace, older indeed than the chapel which was put up in the thirteenth century by Archbishop Boniface. It was in this crypt that the household of Archbishop Laing successfully sheltered during the bombing of the palace. It is appropriate that the archiepiscopal residence should be in danger, for, like other domestic buildings of its original date, it was built to stand up against sudden assault. The gate-tower is strong and sturdy, one of the most perfect examples of an early Tudor gatehouse left in England, as splendid as those of Layer Marney in Essex or of Sissinghurst Castle, mellow in the weald of Kent.

Westminster Hall was as liable to flooding as the cloisters at Lambeth. Holinshed cites two occasions in Henry III's reign when boats could be rowed along the Hall, and after a Tudor flood, in 1579, fish were found gasping on the stone floor. Together with the crypt and the cloisters of St Stephen, Westminster Hall is all that is left of the palace buildings of Westminster, gutted by fire in 1834. It is one of our most precious national possessions. First built by William Rufus in 1097, there was a legend that the Hall had a roof made of Irish bog oak, and that no English spider would ever breed or spin its web among such alien rafters. The structure that we now admire is the creation of Richard II and his master mason, Henry de Yeveley. King Richard ordered the Norman chamber to be made larger, and gave it a tremendous roof with angels holding shields upon the hammer beams, and timber arches springing from stone string courses moulded with the badge of the white hart couchant under a tree. This milky heraldic emblem was the king's badge, based perhaps on that of his mother, the Fair Maid of Kent, which was a white hind : it may, on the other hand, have been chosen as a pun upon his name. The white hart of Richard II is only one of a lovely series of royal badges : the broomcod of Henry II, the silver swan of Henry V, the rose-en-soleil of Edward IV, the portcullis and the sunburst of Henry VIII, Catherine of Aragon's pomegranate.  The hart is still to be seen twice more in London in two places other than the roof of Westminster Hall : it is painted upon the exterior panel of the Wilton Diptych in the National Gallery, and lurks, enormous and clumsy, in a fresco in the triforium of Westminster Abbey.

The wind now blusters coldly through Westminster Hall, for the windows have been smashed by the explosion which twisted Richard Cœur de Lion's sword (his modern statue stands outside St Stephen's porch) and scarred and shattered the balustrading and the glass of that stone pavilion, Henry VII's burial chapel, across the road.  This damage has increased the melancholy aspect of the Hall.  It is usual to think of Westminster Hall in terms of the trial of Charles I, the abdication of Edward II, the deposition of Richard, the condemnation of Lord Strafford :  but these sombre associations are only one side of the medal.  It was the meeting place for the English Law Courts from the thirteenth century to the eighties of the nineteenth :  it was also the scene of many banquets, and its memories are glittering ones :  candle flames and rush-lights casting yellow haloes on green tapestries, the Duke of Lancaster mounting a dais and being acclaimed beneath its gold canopy as Henry IV.  This was in September 1399 :  his coronation, on the feast of St Edward a few weeks later, was the most ostentatious English crowning of the Middle Ages.  The show was perhaps deliberate :  for Richard II was still living in sad prison walls, and the Duke of Lancaster, thirty-two, good-looking, likeable, literate, and fairly able, had no right to the throne.  He himself claimed it, in Westminster Hall in September, as his by conquest, by inheritance, and by Richard's act in handing him the crown.  It was, then, necessary to have an impressive coronation procession, and to win all London to his support.  On the Saturday before his coronation day the Duke proceeded to the Tower of London :  with him, in addition to his usual suite, went forty-six squires, candidates for the honour of knighthood, who spent till Sunday morning, as tradition required, watching their arms.  They were knighted after mass on Sunday, and given long green coats with straight sleeves lined with miniver, and white silk cords and tassels on the left shoulder, by the king.  After dinner on this day the

*Havoc in a placid corner of the Temple: monuments against a wall of the damaged house of the Master. The flat gravestone on the left marks the tomb of Oliver Goldsmith*

*Palace Yard, Westminster, showing the great window,
from Westminster Hall: St. Margaret's Church in the
background*

Duke left the Tower bareheaded, dressed in a German jacket of gold cloth with a French Order of Chivalry about his neck, and accompanied by his retinue and the Prince of Wales. They passed through the city, down streets hung with tapestry, by the nine fountains in the Cheap running with wine. The whole cavalcade, winding past the river palaces (the Palace of the Savoy, for instance, and Baths Inn), down by Whitehall to Westminster, consisted of something like six thousand horse. The next morning another procession entered Westminster Palace : the prelates and clergy from the Abbey, come to conduct the king to his crowning. After confessing, and hearing three masses, the king crossed with them to the Gothic church about nine o'clock and beneath a canopy of blue silk borne on silver staves by four burghers of Calais. At each corner of the canopy was a golden bell, which tinkled in the wind. Inside the Abbey a crimson platform had been set up and upon this a throne of gold. The archbishop proclaimed the king from the four corners of the platform, and then took him to the altar, where he was consecrated, anointed, and crowned. Back in the Hall the company sat down to a banquet, with the king, the two archbishops, and seventeen bishops at the upper table, the great peers at the second, the principal London citizens, the newly created knights, the knights and squires of honour at the other three. It is an enamelled and regal spectacle : yet how hard to visualise as the February wind wafts the thin river mist through the smashed Gothic windows into the present empty darkness of Westminster Hall. During a nineteenth-century restoration of the fabric some musty relics of such feasts were found in a crevice of one of the walls : animals' bones and other remains of food, and the leather sheath of a knife, stamped with the lions passant and the fleur-de-lis.

Without romanticising the Middle Ages, one can safely admit that medieval processions had a theatrical and splendid quality unparalleled in any age. And when it came to coronations, or to royal funerals, they were processions of unimaginable splendour. An outstanding fifteenth-century English funeral was that of Henry V in the Abbey. This military hero, profoundly mourned in England, had died in France of pleurisy, and his embalmed body, wrapped in lead, was drawn in a chariot from the Bois de Vincennes to Calais, by way of Paris, Rouen, and Abbeville. Upon the coffin was the conventional wooden effigy, dressed and painted to simulate life, with a diadem and a sceptre. This jewelled doll was borne along the dusty roads of France, through forests, through fields, over bridges, past churches, by castles and monastic houses, villages and clumps of trees, attended by five hundred men-at-arms clad in black, with black barbed horses, and the butts of their spears turned upward. Twelve captains carried hatchments, and at evening torches were lit, and carried high beside the funeral car: pennons and banners fluttered in the night air. The six horses that drew the chariot were caparisoned each with a different coat-of-arms; the arms of St George, of Normandy, of King Arthur, of Saint Edward, of France, and of England and France together. At Calais the king's body and the ornate dummy were solemnly embarked: and reaching England safely, the procession continued from Dover to London, from London to Westminster. Here Henry V was buried beneath his own chantry chapel in the Abbey. His tomb figure, of wood plated with silver, and with a solid silver head, was stripped at the Reformation.

In peace-time it was always difficult to know how to approach the Abbey. Nowhere in London is there so much to see: but the centuries seemed so mixed up, and unsorted, that though one got an authentic intellection of continuity, one never quite knew what one had come to see. Should one confine oneself for this visit to fifteenth-century tombs, or simply look at the Roubiliacs and the Rysbracks? Or should one scurry round the whole thing? It usually ended with this: the very richness of the Abbey's contents was an invitation to be harum scarum. In a jingling Cromwellian account of the tombs, published in 1658, this temptation to haste is cheerfully expressed. The immediate subject was the wooden funeral figures now in the undercroft:

> Henry the Seventh and his fair queen,
> Edward the First and his queen;
> Henry the Fifth here stands upright,
> And his fair queen was this queen.

> The noble Prince, Prince Henry,
>   King James's eldest son,
> King James, Queen Anne, Queen Elizabeth,
>   And so this chapel's done.

It is a tempo one knows so well : the last few rooms at Fontaine-bleau, the last dungeon at Chillon : the indolent way in which one gulps and gobbles down the past.

In war-time sightseeing in the Abbey is wonderfully simplified. The royal chapels are closed to the public, and peering through the gates they seem more mysterious, as they are certainly more silent and much darker than before. Many of the windows at the east end of the Abbey have been destroyed : and the asbestos that replaces them has created an artificial but romantic gloom. Where once were tombs of ormolu and alabaster we now see efficient sandbag pyramids, throwing great black shadows down the ambulatory floor. And there is the knowledge that inside these protective walls of sandbag the English Middle Ages lie : Henry III, Edward III, Eleanor of Castile, Philippa of Hainault, Richard II, Elizabeth of Bohemia, Henry VII, Elizabeth of York. In the body of the Abbey the eighteenth century still smiles and gestures. Lord Chatham, advancing with his marble hand dramatically upraised, gives them a warning that they do not heed. For these marble throngs are dead throngs : and it is for the living to protect the dead.

The most recent Abbey burial, in October 1940, introduced a fresh note into the solemn traditional procedure. The personages invited to attend the stately funeral of Mr Neville Chamberlain were provided with printed directions on where to shelter in the event of an air attack. Some were to go to the crypt, some to the Norman undercroft, others to the Abbey cloisters. Our century had at last found a practical use for the incidental labyrinths of a great English medieval church.

# II

# THE ATTACK ON WREN'S LONDON

*Ten Wren Churches Burned—Their Appearance—Burned Area of the City—Gunpowder in the Great Fire—The Monument—Church Names—Victorian Destruction of Wren Churches—Ruins of St Bride—of St Andrew-by-the-Wardrobe—Damage to Bow Church—Ruins of St Lawrence Jewry—Ruins of St Vedast Foster—and of Christ Church, Newgate—Lady Digby—Judge Jeffreys buried in St Mary, Aldermanbury—Ruins of this Church —and of St Anne and St Agnes—and of St Alban, Wood Street— and of St Stephen, Coleman Street—Plague Burials—The Plague— Injuries to St Mary-at-Hill—to Dome of St Mary Abchurch—to St Magnus—Fish Street Hill—The Monument Scarred—Bomb Damage in St Paul's—St Paul's and Westminster Abbey—Pedestal of Charles I's Statue—Church of St James, Piccadilly, Wrecked— also St Anne, Soho—Soho Square—Monmouth's House—Lady Dorchester—Roof of Kensington Palace Injured—Wing of Chelsea Hospital Hit—Greenwich Observatory Damaged—Seriousness of Restoration Court—A New Epoch—The Arts of Peace ?*

T HE air-raid damage to Wren's London is greater than that done to the city of the Templars and John Stow. There is far more to destroy. The loss of ten Wren churches in one night is something that made London gasp. The area of the city burned in the evening of 30th December 1940 was small ; but it contained the Guildhall, ten Wren churches, and Allhallows Barking. The newspapers' emphasis on the destruction of the churches was not misplaced, for this was not a calamity felt only by the antiquary and the dilettante. With the latent pride of possession that is a national character- istic (and which Queen Elizabeth's speeches voiced and our nineteenth-century imperialism exemplified), Londoners did care to know that the Wren churches existed, even if they seldom bothered to push their way through the inner swing- doors, and the baize doors behind these, into the comfortable

*St. Bride's Fleet Street: charred beams and calcined pillars in one of Wren's finest churches*

*Interior of St. Bride's Fleet Street in* 1838:
*from Godwin's "Churches of London"*

beauty of St Lawrence Jewry, St Mary Abchurch, or St Peter, Cornhill. The Wren churches were there, as much a part of the City of London as the Mansion House, or the Monument, or Billingsgate Market, or Tower Bridge. They had been built by Wren to replace earlier churches burned in the Fire of London. They had stood within the city for many generations; they would stand there for many more. The destruction of ten of them in one night filled London with anger.

The church ruins that we are now going to consider represent something very remote in time and temper from the Austin Friars and Lambeth Palace Chapel. The Fire of 1666 occurred at an oddly symbolic moment : the higgledy-piggledy hot-blooded life of sixteenth-century London was giving way to the spacious avenues of thought and feeling typified to us by the reign of Queen Anne. The Great Fire swept away the huddled lanes and alleys by the river. It swept away the dark emotional medieval churches : and on their charred sites Wren erected churches like St Lawrence Jewry and St Paul's.

I went round the ten burned churches on the morning after the fire. They had suffered a disgusting change, a metamorphosis at first stupefying. How could these dear interiors, panelled, symmetrical, murky, personal, redolent of the eighteenth century, filled with monuments and busts, urns, tablets, organ cases, carved swags, pulpits and galleries, pews, hassocks, and hymn-books, have been turned into dead bonfires, enclosed by windowless and roofless lengths of wall, with pillars like rotten teeth thrusting up from the heaps of ash ? This was one's immediate reaction. But how soon came recognition, and with this familiarity dismissal, of the banalities of contemporary destruction : the smell of burning, the nude columns, the vacant window-frames, the sagging galleries and melted lead, the sodden piles of roofing, the elaborate doorway that led to the squalid gas-stove devastation of the vestry. I became an amateur in Wren ruins as I had never been an amateur in Wren.

To tabulate the damage to every Wren church in detail would be redundant. It would also be dull. With appropriate modifications the appearance of each ruin is broadly the same. Limits to the variations are set by Christ Church, Newgate, on the one hand, with its vacant expanse of wreckage, by St Anne and St Agnes, Aldersgate (where only the east end has been burned) on the other. There is a norm of desolation, or there was one in the course of the week following on the night of the fires. For some days the church walls steamed and smoked. Underfoot, mounds of dank woodwork (the roof and the galleries tumbled in upon the flaming pews) burned steadily over the vaults. The air quavered with the heat ; the embers of the woodwork sometimes spluttered. But the biggest shock in all the churches was the condition of the pillars. Elegant Doric or Corinthian columns, gilded and plastered, set gracefully between bays, had become barbaric and meaningless in a night. The entablatures they had supported had dissolved. So had the gentle archways, with painted flowers in their soffits, and the globe-cheeked cherubim that looked down from the spandrels. Suspended just above one's head were huge blackened rafters, remains of the sedate galleries (in one church with pretty oval wreaths carved on them, and candlesticks upon each ledge) in which the eighteenth-century world had lolled and whispered during the sermon. The organ, often with an angel or a trumpeting figure of Fame on it, the pulpit under its heavy parasol sounding-board, had disappeared. There was left only the raw stone of the walls (a few broken monuments cemented into them) and the grotesque ranks of calcined pillars, like a forest of totem poles.

Going round the ruins in the burned-out area was anyway a sad performance. The appearance of the streets, at first amazing, melancholy, and splendid, soon ceased to seem at all unusual. Drapers' shops and companies' buildings, put up in that style of modern Romanesque so popular sixty years ago, had come into their own. There they were, long colosseums, with row over row of empty arched windows and tottering preposterously lofty walls. These towering Latin ruins were smoking thickly. At times the quality of the smoke was thin and hardly visible, like jets of steam ; at others it swirled in the wind, and was wafted down the streets. Because many of the city ways are so narrow, the leaning walls seemed to sway and to meet each other at the top. In some streets the buildings had already collapsed into rubble or been dynamited, and what was once a row or an alley had become a barrow of dust and stones. One of the city's most agreeable peculiarities has always been to me the way in which new blocks of offices have been constructed in strict conformity to the old lay-out of curving streets and sinuous lanes and passages. Much of the city of London consists of buildings that are very unimpressive ; yet however clumsy, however vulgar they may individually seem, the atmosphere they create is unchallengeable. Could we find a crude analogy in a house inhabited for centuries, which no redecoration can ever wholly spoil ? Colossal buildings, put up by great vested interests, have been made to curl like serpents to permit the preservation of some tiny alley or lane. Though some of this conservatism should be attributed to the monetary value of all city sites, there is surely a tangible tribute to historical tradition here ?

In some of the burned districts the colour of the city has been changed. Modern concrete, formidable Victorian granite, the tweed-textured walls of earlier buildings (hewn stone speckled by centuries of soot), have been scorched umber. The ruins of Allhallows Barking are chrome yellow. Jutting up from this biscuit desolation the towers and spires of the ten Wren churches are exquisitely white. On the morning after the fire, beams and bell-wheels in the steeples were still smouldering brightly.

The city fire of December 1940 did at one moment look like Pepys' famous description of the fire of 1666. The night sky, lit by a wavering orange glare, seemed to display an aura not at all unlike his " bow of flame." But as we have seen earlier in this commentary, the modern burning was not in any way comparable to the great wall of flame which, like a forest fire in Canada, engulfed the beauties, the riches, and the immemorial associations of old London. In the modern outbreak dynamite was used as gunpowder had been in 1666 to blow up tottering buildings, and to blast a lane in the track of the fire. The use of gunpowder in the Great Fire was largely due to the initiative of Charles II. No single figure connected with the 1666 disaster had a juster claim to recognition than King Charles. By his unexpected energy he saved the city ; by his clear intelligence he managed to combat the growth of childish suspicions about the fire's origin ; by his good sense and vision he successfully supervised the work of reconstruction. These qualities, unusual in a Stuart, were precisely what was needed at that moment ; and for once the seventeenth-century monarchy rose to the occasion. It was perhaps as a tribute to King Charles' performance, as much as in conventional flattery of a royal person, that Wren was so anxious to crown the Monument with a giant statue of him. One of Wren's first designs had been for a pillar with gilt bronze flames spouting from holes along the shaft ; and on the top of this a large phœnix. But he rejected the phœnix as expensive, difficult to understand, and (with its spread wings) a danger in a high wind. The statue of Charles II was his next idea. This suggestion was turned down by the king himself, who preferred " a large ball of metal, gilt," and Wren accordingly proposed the prickly vase of flames that now adorns the column. This vase, when we come to look at it, is far harder to understand from the ground-level than any phœnix could ever have been : it has a vegetable appearance, a gilt thistle or an artichoke high against the London sky. For Wren it had many advantages over the phœnix : he said it could be used for fireworks. Had Charles II sanctioned the statue, we might have had a memorial wholly worthy of that great king, and he would have reigned over the centre of the city of London as does Nelson over Whitehall, or as the Duke of York upon his steps dominates St James's and the Mall.

From the summit of the Monument the city seems peppered with towers and pinnacles. Seen from the cage below the vase of flames, the positions of the churches, indicated by their steeples, used to look oddly haphazard. What other capital city could show such architectural gems as the Wren churches, such cumbrous and magnificent relics of medievalism as St Bartholomew the Great, encased in offices and warehouses ? The most aimless walk down any alley brings one up against the door (how often locked) of a city church : and behind the stone and the railings are those dim exciting interiors, those

48

*Interior of Wren's St. Andrew-by-the-Wardrobe, showing cherubs' heads upon the spandrels: from Godwin's "Churches of London" (1838)*

The burned-out Church of St. Andrew-by-the-Wardrobe. Of the cherubs' heads ornamenting the spandrels only three were saved. A fourth may be seen still in place between the arches

shrines of English history. Here lies Rahere, formal upon his splendid painted tomb; there sits John Stow in life-size terra-cotta, eternally writing with his quill pen perennially renewed. From the chancel wall of St Olave, Hart Street, Mrs Pepys peers down from her bracket, her eyes wide and vivid, her mouth half-open in a nearly whimsical smile. These, and the many like them, made wandering in the city an adventure. And then upon a board outside each church we read its name: and as the ground plan of the modern city differs little from that Hollar drew out in his Map of London after the Great Fire, so the names of all the city churches are medieval, intoxicating. They preserve for us the piety and the topography of Planta-genet and Tudor London. Take the names of a handful of the Wren churches: they form a phonetic cataract: St Nicholas Cole Abbey, St James, Garlickhithe, St Vedast Foster, St Michael Paternoster Royal, St Mary Aldermary, St Andrew-by-the-Wardrobe, St Stephen, Walbrook, St Margaret Pattens, St Mary-le-Bow. But these are medieval in name only: and city churches mean more than Sir Christopher Wren: we cannot ignore the tremendous relics of pre-Stuart London—St Bartholomew the Great with its massive pillars; St Andrew Undershaft, guarded by the pensive figure of John Stow; St Olave, Hart Street; St Helen, Bishopsgate; St Giles, Cripple-gate; Allhallows Barking; the chapel of St Peter ad Vincula in the Tower. All these are churches you could get to know. There is another group (whose numbers are being gradually and sombrely swollen in this war) which had for one that intense appeal, that peculiar mystery of places one could never hope to see: a group composed partly of the churches burned in the Fire of 1666 and not rebuilt, partly of those victims of the nineteenth century, the Wren churches sold up by the Ecclesiastical Commissioners.

Before the Great Fire there were one hundred and thirteen churches in London: of these eighty-nine were computed to have been burnt. Wren himself rebuilt fifty-two: others had vanished for ever, their sites in later years commemorated by blue metal plates. Upon the granite wall of the most im-probable building in the city you may find the inscription, " Site of the Church of St Benet Sherehog," or of St Martin

Pomeroy, or of St Peter at Paul's Wharf, or St Mary Mounthaw, or St Nicholas Acon. These are names that stimulate the imagination as much as references to the rood of St Uncumber in the old Gothic cathedral of St Paul. Their disappearance, however, seems legitimate. Far less numerous, but quite infuriating, are the deliberate destructions (on one pious pretext or another) of the last century. Some of the churches the Victorians ripped down were of the first architectural importance. The church of St Antholin, Budge Row, built by Wren, with eight Roman columns and an oval dome, was demolished in 1874 to make way for Queen Victoria Street. In 1842 St Benet Fink had given place to the Royal Exchange; ten years before this St Michael, Crooked Lane, was sacrificed to the new approach to London Bridge: others— St Mary Somerset, St Mildred, Poultry, St Dionis Backchurch, and St Benet Gracechurch amongst them—were sold under the Bishop of London's Act. How gratifying it must have been to find that the proceeds from the auction sale of Allhallows, Bread Street, were indeed sufficient to build a new church at Poplar (humourlessly given the same name). An earlier, and a more authentic, demolition was that of St Christopher-le-Stocks. This church was pulled down at the time of the Gordon Riots, for its nearness to the Bank made it a potential stronghold for an attack upon that significant building. The decision to abolish St Christopher, though most regrettable, had at least the justification of a species of necessity. Before the Victorians tore down a Wren church, an elaborate (and quite characteristic) service of " deconsecration " would be held in it with the Lord Mayor and the Bishop of London. On one occasion this unctuous ceremony was sadly interrupted by a man who shouted in protest from the nave. But he was a voice crying out in the wilderness of Victorian taste.

The attitude of the last century to many æsthetic questions strikes us as a little unsympathetic. To the Wren churches this attitude was one of hostility. Flaxman gave form to it when he called St Bride's Church in Fleet Street " an ugly thing and better hid." The occasion of this strange statement was an effort on the part of a few enlightened people to keep open a view of the church from the Fleet Street side. This view,

*St. Mary-le-Bow: a wall monument with rosettes, and other fragments from the bombed ceiling, piled before it*

*The listing Western Gallery in St. Vedast Foster*

presented by a fire which burned down some buildings to the south of the church in 1824, was in fact guaranteed to posterity by this generous initiative. Paved, and called St Bride's Avenue, the clearing in Fleet Street gave a reassuring vista of Wren's Portland stone church, serene behind its gateway, with the white octagonal tower like a pagoda which the poet Henley (from its four-tiered diminishing construction) called a " madrigal in stone." Second only to the church of St Stephen, Walbrook, St Bride's is considered to have been one of Wren's masterpieces. It had all the lightness, as well as all the nobility, of St James's, Piccadilly, a lightness emphasised by the comparative absence of modern stained glass. St Bride's hooped windows had escaped the lavish piety of the Victorian patron.

To-day the paved avenue up to St Bride's gives a view of a burned and, superficially, an anonymous building, without a roof, without windows, the churchyard gate locked, the main doorway of the church opening upon a lumpish composition of charred beams and African pillars. Together with St Lawrence Jewry, this church is the worst loss to Londoners and to admirers of Wren. It was finished in 1680, and replaced a largely fifteenth-century structure dedicated to the Irish saint, Brigid, whose head, after so many vicissitudes, was given by the Emperor Rudolf to the Jesuits in Lisbon who keep it still. In this older church a few notabilities were buried : Wynkyn de Worde the printer, who published a second edition of *Malory*, and had a shop in Paul's Churchyard ; and Thomas Sackville, Earl of Dorset ; and Sir Richard Baker. Wynkyn de Worde is a remote and featureless figure, but Thomas Sackville, author of the first English tragedy in blank verse (*Gorboduc*, acted in the Inner Temple in 1561), is a most vivid Elizabethan. It was this brilliant and swarthy courtier who brought to Mary Stuart the news of her sentence to death. Thomas Sackville's bowels only were interred in St Bride's ; in 1649 Sir Richard Baker's body was brought to the church from the Fleet Prison where he had died after whiling away a long imprisonment (for debt) by writing his chronicle of English history. Lovelace, whose lyrics can never lose their freshness or their popularity, was another who was buried in St Bride's vaults, in 1658. The Wren church itself could boast of Samuel Richardson, to whose memory a gravestone was put down in one of the aisles.

The interior of St Bride's had been fiddled about with a good deal since Wren's time. The reredos, for example, was simplified, and the woodwork, once " stone colour," had been changed. Under Queen Anne and the Georges morning prayers in the city churches were offered as early as six or seven o'clock in the morning. Remembering this stray fact which had once caught my attention, I tried, amidst the repulsive wreckage of the burned church, to re-create that placid daily scene, the dignified service as the morning sunlight slipped through the circular clerestory windows, upon the bag-wig of the parson, upon the flowers under the arches, upon the neat galleries, the organ-case, the pulpit and the tablets, upon the curtains above the altar table which in the early eighteenth century were made of scarlet silk with fringes of gold.

St Bride's was the first of the city churches I visited on the day after the fire. The next was St Andrew-by-the-Wardrobe. This church stands at the top of a flight of stone steps, above Queen Victoria Street. The creation of this big street, though it involved the destruction of St Antholin, Budge Row, brought St Andrew's into new prominence. Wren probably never intended this red brick church (with square tower and a white stone parapet round the roof) to occupy such a dominating position. St Andrew's was a very dark church, with galleries: instead of pillars square piers, cased in wood, held up the roof. Between the piers each spandrel was ornamented with a cherub's head and wings. The ceiling was divided into rectangles inside circles, and palm sprigs filled the spaces between. This ceiling, after a night of fire, no longer exists; the copper sheeting from the roof (which has acquired a strange bronzed colour from the fire) lies about the ruins in great bent pieces, a ghastly tarpaulin covering over the remains. One cherub has stayed up on his spandrel: the heads of three more lay at one moment like a clutch of rocs' eggs outside the north door. Away at the east end of the church the metal gates that flanked the altar stood rakishly crooked in the piles of ash. In a corner was the bust of a former rector, still surmounting his marble memorial

*St. Lawrence Jewry after the Fire: the porch of the Guildhall visible through a window of the smouldering Church*

*A Seventeenth-Century Church Monument:*
*the Halliday Memorial in St. Lawrence Jewry*

*St. Lawrence Jewry before the Fire: the west end, showing the organ-case*

*The Vestry, with its baroque woodwork and ceiling by Thornhill*

*A Week Later: St. Lawrence Jewry under Snow*

pyramid against the wall. The window just above his head had been mangled by blast, and the leading was twisted like barbed wire.

St Andrew-by-the-Wardrobe was a church I have very often visited. It was one I liked and knew well. Once known as St Andrew-juxta-Castle Baynard, it took its present name from the proximity of the Wardrobe Tower. This tower was built by Sir John Beauchamp in the first half of the fourteenth century. At Sir John Beauchamp's death his executors sold the strong house to the king, Edward III, and it was made into a place of storage for ceremonial robes, both royal ones and those belonging to the Garter Knights. Later, robes were actually made in the Wardrobe, and later still (in the Wars of the Roses), books were bound in the tower. It is agreeable to pause and think of this, even in the ruins of St Andrew's Church. The Renaissance first flowered in England (which means in London) under Edward IV, and those bindings that were an essential part of the new magnificent princely households (that of Humphrey, Duke of Gloucester, for instance) were made for the king here. We have records of some of Edward IV's books bound in the Wardrobe Tower; *Livy*, *The Bible*, Froissard's *Chronicles*, *Josephus' History*, and *The Fortress of Faith*. The *Josephus* is preserved in London to-day, in the Soane Museum in Lincoln's Inn Fields: an ostentatiously lovely illuminated copy, with the Royal Arms upon the borders. Also near the Wardrobe Tower stood the church of St Anne, Blackfriars, within the precincts of the Dominicans: burned in the Fire, this church was not rebuilt, and the parish was linked with that of St Andrew.

It is a relief to turn from these two churches, totally destroyed, to one that is battered but not open to the sky. The most famous of all London churches, in Stow's day St Mary-le-Bow owed its enormous prestige to the many accidents that had befallen it since the eleventh century; in ours its reputation is due to Wren and to the bells. The earlier church, square-towered and pinnacled, collapsed in the Great Fire. Bow Bells, however, have continued to ring down the centuries, and every-one knows that a true Cockney must be born within their sound. In the Civil Wars of the fifteenth century the Bow Bell was rung each night at nine o'clock. The Cheapside prentices, indignant at the unreliability of this curfew, composed their strange couplet and sang it out upon the evening air :

> Clerk of the Bow Bell with the yellow locks,
> For thy late ringing thy head shall have knocks.

To which the bellringer was fancied to reply :

> Children of Cheap hold you all still,
> For you shall have the Bow Bell rung at your will.

Is there not some quality, quite ominous, quite indefinable, lurking in the first and fourth of these lines that raises them from depths of doggerel to the mystic levels of poetry ? A brusque contrast, illustrating all the same the continuity of sentiment about Bow Bells, comes with Alexander Pope :

> Far as loud Bows stupendous Bells resound.

This is the eighteenth century in a nutshell. As wide a distance separates Pope from the rhyming prentices and the York and Lancaster emblems as lies between the melodious pealing of the new bells swung in Wren's campanile from the hollow clangor of the medieval curfew. It is to the world of the curfew that one feels drawn to-day—the period of the Pastons, when English life was exposed to that anarchy and property to those many dangers which Pope's compact, veneered century had helped us to forget.

To Stow's authorities the very existence of Bow Church was surprising. It had been such an unlucky place. A Norman gale had blown the roof away, and hurled rafters deep into the ground. In the twelfth century the steeple was burned down in the course of a street brawl. In the thirteenth a fresh steeple fell and killed people below. Between these two accidents a murder had been committed in St Mary's. And so it went on until the Great Fire of 1666, when the whole medieval church subsided in smoke. The old bad fortune of the church has not persisted to-day. Though knocked about in the bombing of the Cheapside area Wren's church remains upright, with its spire unshaken, its roof smashed, its box-like structure chipped.

*Christ Church Newgate:*
*east and west aspects*

63

*Christ Church Newgate:
Wren's Church upon the
site of the Greyfriars,
to-day and in 1838*

The windows have been blown in. But here is no heap of rubble, no blackened shell : and no occasion for the Londoner's lament. Cheapside is the scene of some rather spectacular bits of damage. One can stand against the wall of St Mary-le-Bow and gaze at the great dome of the Cathedral over a foreground of charred shops. St Mary's used to be a hidden church, overshadowed by later buildings, but now it has obtained a new dignity in its desolate surroundings, with its blind and its windowless walls.

We return to the burned-out churches. There are eight more, and again we get an harmonious sequence of names : St Augustine-with-St Faith ; St Lawrence Jewry ; Christ Church, Newgate ; St Alban, Wood Street ; St Mary, Aldermanbury ; St Stephen, Coleman Street ; St Anne and St Agnes ; St Vedast Foster. Amongst these the destruction of St Lawrence Jewry is a crushing blow. St Lawrence was a splendid and slightly foreign-looking church, standing near the Guildhall, and with more command in its situation than most of the churches Wren was commissioned to build. As the name suggests, the old church of St Lawrence was in a ghetto district. In medieval history a ghetto often meant a pogrom, and under Henry III there was a massacre of Jews close to St Lawrence Church. But though Sir Thomas More preached in the old church, it is of the Wren building, so sumptuous, so spectacular, that it is appropriate to think. It was the most costly of all the new churches, and contained specimens of seventeenth-century carved panelling unrivalled in this country. The vestry was rich with swags, with fruit and flowers and wreaths of oak, and in a quatrefoil upon the plaster ceiling was a decorative painting by Thornhill. The doorways leading to the vestibule and the tower were splendid. Each pediment was broken to permit a wooden angel to stand there, with a palm branch in her hand ; between the doorways was the organ, aloft upon Corinthian columns. It is perhaps the adjective, with its double meaning, that makes one think of a wooden angel as something medieval : a stiff, formalised figure in a French cathedral, with rigid drapery and thin stylised hands. The angels of St Lawrence Jewry, however, were the epitome of Baroque Christianity : florid, ornate creatures, elegant in their liquid draperies, living, flamboyant, with curling feathers in their great enveloping wings. Under the organ case the wooden pillars stood in a group like motionless courtiers : there was a theatrical grandeur about them, the Caroline classicism of Dryden's *All for Love*. Here is indeed a major architectural loss.

A seventeenth-century prelate of real importance was closely connected with St Lawrence Jewry. This was John Tillotson, who died Archbishop of Canterbury. Tillotson began his career as a leading Presbyterian, and had even married Cromwell's niece in the old church of St Lawrence in 1664. In the same year he was appointed Tuesday Lecturer in St Lawrence, and his sermons, novel for their logic and their lucidity in that age of embroidered eloquence, made him a fashionable figure. He would preach from the pulpit upon every subject : even urging rich ladies to nurse their babies themselves and to avoid lavishing expensive christening presents upon hired nurses. With Bishop Burnet he attended Lord William Russell on the scaffold in 1683, and his continued friendship with the widow, Rachel Lady Russell, brought him the confidence of the Princesses Mary and Anne. He was especially intimate with both King William and Queen Mary, and would pace the newly panelled galleries of Kensington Palace, discussing politics, discoursing on the soul. William III made him Clerk of the Closet and Dean of St Paul's. When Sancroft ceased to be Archbishop (on his refusal to take the oath to the usurpers), Tillotson was selected in his stead. He was not particularly anxious to take up office, and managed to get the confirmation deferred till the spring of 1691. In November 1694 he died, and was buried by his wife in the new church of St Lawrence Jewry. The monument she put up to him, on the north wall, has come through the fire rather well.

Other monuments have survived the fire in St Lawrence Jewry. The most lovely of these is that to a lady called Brown, who stands upright on her bracket much as Lady Grace Pierrepoint stands surveying the ruins of St Anne's, Soho. The fire has increased the beauty of this Queen Anne statue : for molten lead has run down over her, and clings silver to her

*The Main Door of the Church of
St. Mary the Virgin, Aldermanbury*

*The Wren Church of St. Anne*
*and St. Agnes, Aldersgate*

hair, her shoulders, and her arms, giving a falsely festive air. The same effect of inappropriate Christmas decorations was to be seen upon the big monuments to Nelson and others in the shell of the Guildhall. Opposite to this lady in St Lawrence's, at the other end of the church, was a fine alabaster of a man in a wheel ruff. This bust has been beheaded, and the lady beside it has been scalped. Her forehead, with three curls on it, lay amongst the ashes, with a part of an alabaster skull from the same memorial, and the head of the man in the ruff. This head had broken vertically as it fell. The face had come cleanly away from the rest, and it lay there helplessly upon the ground, staring up at one, an expressionless face with a small beard, unnervingly like the conventional Shakespeare.

St Lawrence, the Gridiron Martyr, never had more than two churches dedicated to him in London. There was St Lawrence Jewry and St Lawrence Poultney, but this last was not built again after the fire. St Vedast, the patron saint of the next church we must consider, however, had only one other church in the whole of England. This sixth-century ecclesiastic, who baptised King Clovis, was well known in churches across the Channel, but almost forgotten here. His body lies in Arras Cathedral, and his name, in France corrupted to St Vaast, in Flanders to St Waast, became in London, St Foster. The Wren church of St Vedast Foster, of which hardly anything remains, was famous for the beauty of its spire. The spire is still there, and with it the great west window, an exquisitely brittle palm spray in relief above it. The gallery under this window and the pillars holding the gallery up are burned, but standing : the roof collapsing on to them has made the whole thing slip forwards and sag.

Far more interesting, but interesting for its associations, is the wide Italianate building, Christ Church, Newgate. This large church, which Wren fitted over the site of the choir of the Greyfriars Church, has been more thoroughly destroyed than any other. It was a noble but unexciting specimen of Wren : with a spacious groined roof, a great deal of wainscoting, a great many pews. After the Dissolution of the Greyfriars house Henry VIII converted the church into a parish church, and pulled down St Nicholas Flee Shambles and St

Ewins to endow it. Christ Church was burned out in the Great Fire, and among the funerary monuments then lost was the ornate memorial put up by Sir Kenelm Digby to his wife, the immortal Venetia, who died in 1633. Venetia Digby was born in 1600, and died when she was thirty-three : leaving a circle of admirers who realised suddenly what rarity they had been privileged to know. Many elegies were written upon her. Her beauty has been perpetuated by Van Dyck in several portraits, and a well-known picture shows her lying in her bed. Ben Jonson produced his series, *Eupheme*, in her memory :

> A mind so pure, so perfect fine,
> As 'tis not radiant but divine ;
> And so disdaining any tryer,
> 'Tis got where it can try the fire.

> There high exalted in the Sphere,
> As it another Nature were,
> It moveth all and makes a flight
> As circular as infinite.

>         .        .        .        .        .

> The voice so sweet, the words so fair,
> As some soft chime had stroked the air,
> And, though the sound were parted thence,
> Still left an echo in the sense.

Her death was sudden, and to Sir Kenelm heartbreaking. A renowned scientific amateur, it was natural that an unkind rumour should attribute her death to him : he had made her, people said, drink viper wine to preserve her beauty, and the draught had been fatal. The widower retired to Gresham College for two years, in a mourning cloak, a high cornered hat, and with the appearance, says Aubrey, of a hermit. When he died many years afterwards, he had directed that his body should be laid in his wife's tomb in the long dim nave of Christ Church, but that no mention of him should be cut upon the monument.

After the Great Fire, Christ Church was left to stand ruinous on into the eighties. Funerals, though, were held amongst the rubble. In 1681 the wife of that heroic figure Richard Baxter, the Nonconformist, was "buried in the ruins, in her own mother's grave. The grave was the highest next to the old altar." In his years of agonised persecution she had been an enormous comfort to her husband, a man outstanding for his intransigeance in a shifting moment of history. Baxter would talk monarchy to Cromwell, and then refuse a bishopric (the pink stone one of Hereford) from Charles the Second. The result, not surprisingly, was that he became anathema to all parties. In 1686, as an old man, he came into contact with Judge Jeffreys of the Bloody Assize, who is said to have threatened him with a whipping at the cart's tail. However violently one may feel about James II's brutal Chief Justice (and any knowledge of the Bloody Assize country in Somerset, where hatred of him lingers still, must make one violent), one should perhaps remember how abominably painful was his death. At the flight of James II in 1688 Jeffreys was caught as he was trying to escape, disguised as a seaman, from Wapping Stairs : almost lynched by the frenzied crowd, he died in the Tower, though of natural causes. Not only was Jeffreys' death as humiliating and as painful as any he had ordered for his victims : his body (last indignity ?) has disappeared. After more than four years' burial in the Tower of London, the corpse was handed over to Jeffreys' family, who interred it in the church of St Mary, Aldermanbury. In the nineteenth century a house was still shown as the residence of Jeffreys when Common Serjeant ; a large family house, standing near the east end of St Mary's Church, with an oak staircase and parquet floors. The church registers contain entries of baptisms of members of the Jeffreys family, and of Christiania, a daughter of the judge. Hatchments, banners, his sword, gauntlets, and spurs could be seen hanging on the church walls in Queen Anne's time, but these insignia are long pulled down. The actual body, in its coffin in 1810, was nowhere to be found during the restoration of 1863. It may yet be lying somewhere in the vaults; it may have lain there during the night of 30th December 1940, when the church above it was blazing away. The stone pineapples at the gate of St Mary, Aldermanbury, have crashed to the ground. In the churchyard a mediocre bust of William Shakespeare (commemorating the burial in the church of

Heminge and Condell, his fellow actors and legatees) surveys the damaged area from the midst of some dirty shrubs. On the shrubs and in the branches of the trees by the church bits of rag and office files shivered in the wind.

We shall consider three more burned Wren churches in the city: St Anne and St Agnes, Aldersgate; St Stephen, Coleman Street; and St Alban, Wood Street. The first of these is the least damaged of all the burned churches. It is also the least architecturally interesting. A small, prettily proportioned church, its effect is spoiled by the colouring of the plaster walls, the pillars, and the ceiling—light green and sugar pink. The quiet and unpresuming character of St Anne's Church has not been changed by the fire, which only burned the altar and the east end. The rest of the church is sodden but unharmed: a doll's chapel dipped into a pail of water. The church's only charm, to my mind, lay in its original name: St Anne in the Willows, and in Stow's gloss on this, that no willows grew in the graveyard in his time, " wherein only do grow some tall ash trees." And the churchyard still has this leafy atmosphere: in the middle of summer, when dust blew along St Martin le Grand, and Gresham Street reeked of petrol fumes, this church-yard, and the adjacent one of the old church of St John Zachary, were islands of shadow, still and cool.

St Alban's Church, Wood Street, which is close to St Anne and St Agnes, used to be cited as a dubious example of Wren's Gothic, or, as he liked to call it, " Saracenic " style. There was always the probability that the lay-out of the church was not by Wren at all. In 1632 the old church of St Alban was found to be unsafe, and Inigo Jones, reporting on its state, recommended that it should be pulled down " or it would suddenly prevent that labour and fall to the ground itself." Inigo Jones rebuilt the church, and it may be that St Alban's, not altogether destroyed in the Great Fire, was only patched and pulled about by Wren.

I really have no memory whatever of the interior of St Alban's, Wood Street. Looking at wreckage becomes very blurring. One's clearest recollection of a church gets overlaid with the refuse of destruction, just as the gravestones in the aisles of a burned church are lost beneath piles of ash and

*Fallen Roofing in St. Anne and St. Agnes*

*St. Paul's Cathedral: masonry flung from the
sanctuary roof lies before the Tijou Gates*

smouldered wood. The fittings of St Alban's had been much modernised, the pews had been cut down, the pulpit's sounding board lost. The reredos had gone too. Although one had never seen this reredos, it is upon it that I fixed my mind. An eighteenth-century description makes it sound so shimmering and lovely. It was designed with four fluted columns, upon each of which a lamp with a gilt taper was carved. Between the columns were the Ten Commandments, set out in golden letters upon a black ground. To north and south of the Commandments were, as usual, the Lord's Prayer and the Creed, in gold on blue. Above the Commandments was a " glory " between cherubim, and over the cornice the queen's arms, with the crest and enriched helmet, and the supporters propping it up. Like the red silk curtain in St Bride, Fleet Street, in 1708, this flash of gold on black, of gold on blue, and the curvilinear qualities of the achievement, serve to form a coloured picture in one's mind.

The last burned church, St Stephen, Coleman Street, is memorable for its connection with the Great Plague of 1665. This hideous calamity, which fortunately preceded the Great Fire (what would have happened had the Plague broken out after the fire, among the wailing refugees sleeping on carts in Bunhill Fields ?), is something which is happily unlikely to occur again. As an experience of horror, it beat the Great Fire hollow ; it also, in my opinion, beat the bombings of 1940. To have lived through the Great Plague seems to me as remarkable a feat (though not as questionable a one) as that of an ancestor of my own who lived through the Black Hole of Calcutta. By being the biggest of London epidemics of the Plague, the 1665 outbreak has come to seem the only one. A glance at the records, or the letters of any earlier period and any earlier reign, however, show what a constant menace the Plague was felt to be ; it gave an insecurity to daily life, to which the Germans have now reintroduced us. The really curious fact about the Great Plague is that once it had subsided there was no similar outbreak again in England. The cessation was glibly attributed to the Great Fire : but in every other city in England the Plague ceased at about the same time. In Western Europe, generally, the closing years of the seventeenth century saw the disappearance of the Plague. It left Spain in 1681 and Germany in 1683 (though it recurred here in one solitary outbreak in 1707). In London in 1665 the havoc was terrific. The mortality (probably underestimated) rose from 43 in May to 31,000 in September, the peak month: nearly 69,000 people died in London, over a sixth of the city's population. Evacuees from London helped to spread the Plague all over England. Rich landowners were taxed for relief funds, and some of them, the Russells, for instance, gave generously to erect pesthouses.

St Stephen's Church had important documents and registers of plague burials. There was a story that the under-sexton of the church (which was situated in the very heart of the contaminated area) would go round all alone with a hand-cart collecting the bodies, loading his barrow with the discoloured and infectious dead. He contracted no illness from this pursuit, and lived for another twenty years. The interior of the church of St Stephen, Coleman Street, had been so altered as to have little obvious connection with Sir Christopher Wren.

As much remodelled as St Stephen's is the church of St Mary-at-Hill, reconstructed in 1849. St Mary-at-Hill has been injured by bomb explosions near to it: so has the lovely domed St Mary Abchurch. The damage to the cupola frescoes (by Thornhill) in St Mary Abchurch, practically amounts to demolition: for bomb blast has torn down great pieces of the painted plaster, and the whole interior, once so graceful and airy, is filled with scaffolding and flaking wall surface. Contrasted with the fire's devastation, normal bomb damage like that to St Mary-at-Hill, St Mary Abchurch, and the big church of St Magnus the Martyr seems tame.

St Magnus, London Bridge, has not, though, escaped fire in its time. In 1760 a nearby oilshop caught alight and burned the church roof. The present appearance of the church, from the outside, is comforting, for only the windows are gone: inside it seems strapped and held together by a network of scaffolding and steel struts. It is the superb tower, and not the interior of St Magnus, that makes it so notable a Wren church. It stands at the bottom of Fish Street Hill, below the Monument.  Fish Street Hill is a very early byway: "Up Fish Street Hill ! Down St Magnus Corner !" is a noisy cry in one of the parts of Henry VI (I forget which), and Stow noted that the Black Bell Inn on the hill was traditionally a residence of the Black Prince.  The smell of the hill has been noted for centuries.  To-day it still seeps up from Billingsgate Fish Market, where the porters scurry by with herring boxes balanced on their round hard leather hats (a survival, it is always said, of medieval hats).  In the seventeenth century the ascent of Fish Street Hill was a great deal sharper, far too sharp for carriage horses.  People in carriages were often obliged to get out, and if it were at night to send for a link to light them up the muddy street.  When the city was replanned after the Fire, care was taken to make the hill's gradient less atrocious, and even Evelyn thought it "become very easy and pleasant." Upon the top of the hill was placed the Monument ; ill-placed, thought Evelyn, who would have preferred the pillar to stand in the Cheap, and could not see why it was put up where the Fire began, and not where it was stopped.

So far the Monument has got through the bombing unhurt. The relievo on the pediment is gashed by splinters.  This lovely and pedantic composition by the father of Colley Cibber shows Charles II in Roman clothes advancing to the aid of a nymph representing London, lying disconsolately on her ruins.  The king is attended by the Duke of York, by the Sciences, by Liberty ("waving a hat"), by Architecture, Fortitude, and Justice : in the right-hand corner lies Envy, scowling upwards, with flames in its mouth, gnawing on a heart.  In the left background is the Fire and the amazed citizens, in the right background the reconstruction of the city is in progress.  When you have stared your fill at this scene, you can wander round the Monument and gaze up till you are dizzy at the central column and at the four weathered dragons on the corners of the base.  At the peak of the Popish Plot frenzy in 1681 the Court of Aldermen commanded that an English inscription be added to the Latin ones upon the faces of the Monument, accusing the Catholics of a deliberate attempt to fire the city.  With James II's accession the anti-papist lines were quickly erased, only to be cut deeper in the reign of William III.  They were at last removed by an Act of the Common Council in January 1831.

No sooner was the Monument completed than it became an object of acute interest. Sir Dudley North, the Caroline financier and advocate of Free Trade, who had made his fortune in Turkey in the sixteen-sixties, was one of the many who liked to climb the black marble steps in the hollow column and emerge through the metal vase at the top. Standing there with a friend or with his son Roger ("I cannot describe how hard it was to persuade ourselves that we stood safe," the son adds) Sir Dudley would genially observe the river and the city spread out beneath him, and contrast the Monument with the mosques and towers he had seen in Smyrna and Constantinople. In the eighteenth century the Monument was immensely popular. People in the neighbouring taverns would bet upon the speed with which a boy could run up to the top and down again. In 1730 the drawer of the Baptist Head performed this feat in two and a half minutes. There was another spectacle, called "flying from the Monument," in the news-sheets; for this some agile person (often a sailor) would slide head first down a rope tied round the top of the column on to a heap of feather beds in Monument Yard. A different kind of spectacle was afforded by a series of suicides from the balcony of the Monument. The unhappy person would fling himself down from the pillar, splitting his head open upon a corner of its base.

It is not now possible, with war conditions, to enter and climb the Monument. We may look forward to this as one of the minor pleasures of peace. In such context a passage from Wilkinson's *Londina Illustrata* has a sad topicality: "The Monument was erected by an architect of such consummate skill," he writes, "and constructed upon such certain and scientific principles that it may be regarded as secure from every attack, excepting the shock of an earthquake." The conclusion is not for me to draw.

\*     \*     \*     \*

I shall never forget the strange effect of being within the crypt of St Paul's Cathedral one morning when the fire ruins in Newgate Street were being blown up by dynamite. The

78

The Interior of St. Alban Wood Street in
1838: from Godwin's "Churches of London"

*The Rector returns to his Church: the
burned interior of St. Alban Wood Street*

explosions were far louder than any thunder, and the Cathedral fabric trembled solemnly with the burst. I was standing at the east end of the crypt, near the Tudor alabaster figures, charred relics of the old cathedral destroyed in the Fire of 1666. Years ago, when I first noticed these calcined Elizabethans, they seemed infinitely less apropos than they have come to seem now. Theirs was a past and not a personal tragedy : a tragedy of London churches burning, of a dramatic but remote calamity that one could read of in Clarendon or in Pepys. But now touring the ruins of ten Wren churches, I had spent a morning looking at burned effigies far more modern than these, and now that the Baroque, the Palladian, the Regency, and the Victorian in monumental imagery have endured the same horrors as the Renaissance Carews and old Sir Nicholas Bacon in the crypt of St Paul's, these inflexible Tudor tomb-figures seem to offer a rigid consolation, and to provide a kind of continuity (though a ghastly one) for the stone and marble victims of the incendiary bomb.

The damage to the east end of St Paul's Cathedral is more severe than it looks. A bomb exploding in the roof has hurled part of a great arch down upon the altar (pulverising this tasteless Victorian creation, but missing the equally ugly reredos). For many days colossal pieces of gilded masonry (some with fragments of mosaic stuck to them) lay strewn about the altar steps in the half light of the Cathedral. This grandiose litter had the majesty of a Piranesi ; one thought of Gibbon and not of Wren. At present the toppling reredos is held together by a complex structure of scaffolding, and gives one the illusion that this end of the Cathedral is not quite finished. One expects to see Wren, with his long sensitive face and his pale wig, strutting along the chancel : or pulled up (the Duchess of Marlborough called it " dragged up ") the pillars in a basket, as he was three or four times a week, to inspect the progress of the work. The stones that have fallen from the roof of the choir have been sorted into neat rows : they add to the general feeling of incompleteness. To apply such wishful imagining to the results of bombardment is wrong and ridiculous : but after a tour of the burned churches this particular illusion is one it is agreeable to indulge.

81

St Paul's Cathedral can be taken as the embodiment of English history for the last two centuries: Westminster Abbey provides the rest. About the Abbey we feel far more intimately, far more deeply. It contains a thousand individual memories, and its steps and chantries are potentially thronged with personages we cannot even think of in St Paul's : Henry VI peering down from a gallery, Elizabeth Woodville seeking sanctuary, Mary Tudor on her knees before St Edward's relics, Anne Boleyn being crowned (her black hair combed out over the gold tissue), Queen Elizabeth's funeral cortège, Buckingham in his bay of Henry VII's chapel. But for the centuries since the Stuarts, for space and solemnity, for symmetry and style, you must turn to St Paul's. To-day that unparalleled interior can give us something of momentous value : for by displaying the necessity (and simultaneously the grandeur) of true unity in architecture, does it not suggest the importance of this principle in other and more animated spheres ?

\*     \*     \*     \*

Going from the Cathedral westwards to the shattered church of St James, Piccadilly, the damage at Chelsea Hospital, and the tumbled roofing of Kensington Palace, one inevitably passes through Trafalgar Square. Trafalgar Square often seems the focal point of the whole of London. To-day, with its traffic jams and its busy crowds, there is no indication that this is the heart of a city subjected to the worst bombardment in history. Except for the long brick shelters by the fountains and the war-savings slogans about the base of Nelson's column, there is no suggestion of the war here. At Charing Cross, however, we may notice an unexpected igloo of sandbags covered with corrugated iron. The position of this structure seems familiar : and then we realise that beneath it is concealed the world-famous statue of Charles I on horseback, riding on a fine pedestal, itself one of Wren's least known works. This equestrian king will come through any bombing : I suspect that, in his strong tin hut, he would survive even the collapse of the column in the centre of the square. Cast in 1633 in a piece of ground near Covent Garden Church, from the designs of Le Sueur, this statue of Charles I was never put up in a public place till the Restoration. Under the Commonwealth it was sold to a brazier on the strict understanding that he would break the brass horse and rider into fragments : in reality he buried them underground, and showed miscellaneous pieces of metal to the authorities to convince them that he had done as they wished. In 1674 the statue was bought by the Crown and set upon its Wren pedestal : the stonework was executed by Joshua Marshall, who held the post of Master Mason to Charles II which Henry de Yevele had occupied to Richard II. Two sketches for the pedestal lie among the Wren papers preserved at Oxford.

Perhaps because of its situation St James's, Piccadilly, was the most popular of all Wren's smaller churches. It has been almost entirely destroyed. Built in 1680, it was paid for by Henry Jermyn, Earl of St Albans, the supposed second husband of Henrietta Maria. Lord St Albans owned the estate upon which in his lifetime St James's Square was (most profitably) constructed. Early engraved views of St James's Square, with its low buildings and pavement pegged off by wooden posts, show that St James's was intended to bear a more direct relation to it than the rebuilt Duke Street and Jermyn Street now permit. Like Soho Square (" the great square " of Evelyn, who used to bring his family to winter there), St James's Square seems especially characteristic of late Stuart life : when the great cuffs of men's coats turned back, stiff with embroidery, and their perukes were heavy and formal, and ladies wore knotted fontanges ribbons on their heads and rattled the sticks of painted fans. St James's Church, at the top of Duke Street, must have seemed to preside over St James's Square : the engravings show it sitting there at the end of the little steep street, very neat and severe, but homely, like a wooden Noah's Ark. Wren had economised over the exterior : but the inside was gorgeous with carving and marbles, galleries and pews. Pottering in to see the new church one day in December of 1684, Evelyn was bewitched to find how elegant it was ; the altar, with its Gibbons' garlands and its wonderful plate, seemed to him more beautiful than any other in England, " nor has there been any abroad more handsomely adorned." Wren himself would cite the inside of St James's as an example of what a church interior should be. Without walls of a second order, without lantern and buttresses, he thought it " beautiful and convenient, and as such the cheapest form of any I could invent." The carvings in St James's, unlike those of St Lawrence Jewry, were removed to safety before the church was bombed.

St James's, Piccadilly, shared with St Anne's, Soho, the patronage of the people of quality. St Anne's Church, quite burned out, is not a work of Wren : but the fact of its having been put up at the same time as St James's, and in the style of architecture which Wren favoured, warrant its inclusion here. St James's Church was named in compliment to the Duke of York : St Anne's in compliment to his daughter the Princess Anne. In the case of the Soho church the compliment was possibly emphasised by the plan of the church tower (taken down in 1802), said to have been copied from one in Copenhagen ; for in 1683 Anne had married Prince George of Denmark. St Anne's, Soho, was consecrated by the Bishop of London (though in an uncompleted state) in 1686, its parish, like that of St James, being carved out of that of St Martin-in-the-Fields. Before St Anne was finished Soho Square had been laid out, and people of importance began to congregate there for the winter. The chief house in the square was the imposing mansion of the Duke of Monmouth, to whom his father, Charles II, had granted the Soho property, and who later made Soho the word of the day upon the mournful water-meadows of Sedgemoor. The Monmouth house, pulled down in the later eighteenth century, was very impressive. Through fine iron gates, surmounted by a ducal coronet and supported by big stone piers, you could look into the paved carriage courtyard : inside the house was a mass of gilding—gold birds on the blue satin walls of the main first-floor room, gilded beading in the shutters, mirrors in gilt frames between the windows, classical busts—Seneca, Trajan, Caracalla—on the huge staircase, which had very low treads and patterned parquetry landings. The Duchess of Monmouth was one of St Anne's parishioners : but so was the pale, ugly Lady Dorchester, the mistress of the Duke of York, and hope of the anti-papist party. Lady

*St. James' Piccadilly: the Church which Wren himself described as "beautiful and convenient," and which became the most fashionable place of worship in eighteenth-century London*

*The East Window of St. Anne's Soho,
showing the figure of Lady Grace Pierrepont*

Dorchester was the object of several of Lord Dorset's spiteful satirical verses :

> Tell me, Dorinda, why so gay,
>   Why such embroidery, fringe, and lace ?
> Can any dresses find a way
> To stop th' approaches of decay,
>   And mend a ruin'd Face ?

On the Duke of York's accession as James II she was moved to a house in St James's Square and took a pew in St Anne's, Soho.

The shell of St Anne's, Soho, was, last winter, the most melancholy and so the loveliest of all the air-raid ruins. The hooped east window, jagged and empty, looked out on to Dean Street, and the marble figure of Lady Grace Pierrepoint, the octogenarian daughter of one of Charles I's followers, stares out through it at the street life of Soho. The figure has lost its arm, its canopy, and the curtain at its back ; but poised upon its drum-shaped bracket, it has remained upright. Beneath the barley-sugar pilasters of this monument we may observe two tiny but triumphant skulls, grinning death's-heads that have successfully eluded fire and blast.

When Princess Anne was living at Berkeley House she would attend service at St James's, Piccadilly. It was in this church, the Duchess of Marlborough states in her memoirs, that a deliberate insult to the princess was planned. During her period of disfavour with King William and Queen Mary, her brother-in-law and sister, orders were sent to the Rector of St James to refuse any marks of respect to the Princess Anne. The text was not to be laid out upon her cushion, she was to be treated like anybody else. The rector replied that he would do nothing without written orders, which were not forthcoming : and so, the Duchess triumphantly concludes, nothing came of this intrigue. Whether there is any special reason to believe the Duchess of Marlborough on this more than on other points one does not know : in any case her influence with Princess Anne, a lymphatic and quarrelsome person, was seldom directed towards healing the breach between that wheezing royalty and the king and queen. Both St James and St Anne, then, had fashionable congregations : and how hard the preachers were put to it to find sermons for this pernickety audience. Mr Wake would preach to his noble parishioners in St Anne's on the necessity for taking up the cross and behaving themselves "strenuously" in times of persecution—a sly and welcome reference to the slightly aggressive Catholicism of King James II. But Mr Wake's congregation, like that of his colleague in St James, was not composed of people eager to shoulder the cross : lolling in the box pews, daydreaming in the galleries, they do not look to us as though they were inflamed by any intense religious zeal. Their Christianity was demure and simplified : it was also smart, and like all smart or fashionable emotions it was shallow, sterile, and dry.

\* \* \* \*

Kensington Palace, eternally linked with the names of William and Mary, and with memories of Queen Caroline, has been hit in the air raids : and though the long south front, flat pilasters, eleven windows and all, is unharmed, the windows at the eastern end of the palace have been blown out, and a part of the roof and some of the small rooms of the building have been gutted. In the war Kensington Palace seems especially gloomy and deserted ; secluded amidst its dank shrubberies of evergreen, with frigid vistas between the park trees, the round pond given over to winter and the gulls, everywhere dampness and gaping window-frames. This damp atmosphere is most inappropriate to the palace : for King William bought it from Lord Nottingham in the hope that its dry air would improve his asthma after the riverside moisture of Whitehall. The old house of Lord Nottingham was enlarged by Wren, who concocted a dark but suitable small residence for the king and queen. Up and down these narrow galleries Queen Mary wandered, in these lofty lonely rooms King William yearned for Holland, and felt sickly, and coughed and coughed. George I commissioned Kent to improve the palace ; the great frescoed staircase dates from his reign. Queen Caroline would sit in her apartments at Kensington gossiping to Lord Hervey, and here, most inexplicably, Queen Victoria managed to pass a merry chintz childhood, and to emerge unsoured from these sombre rooms. A picture in the Dulwich

Gallery shows Princess Victoria as she must have been at Kensington : a round, gay little child in a beaver hat.

The Hospital for Chelsea Pensioners has always seemed to me a more properly palatial building than Kensington Palace. If Chelsea Hospital were less majestic one would be tempted to call it rambling, for it covers an immense expanse of ground, with its two quadrangles and big court open to the river, its outbuildings and subsidiary houses on either side. I stood one morning recently beneath the colonnade that runs the full length of the south front (with its brave Latin inscription telling how the hospital was begun by Charles II, continued by James II, and brought to perfection under William and Mary). It was a very misty January morning and an air raid was in progress. Somewhere up in the sky shells were bursting : the guns bellowed far down the river, and sometimes a burst seemed to be right over one's head. The river mist hung about the court-yards, about the purple brick walls, the white stone pediments and cornices, about the broken windows, the clock turret, and the Doric portico, about the dwarf lime trees and the avenues of horse chestnut. Straight before me was the river, hidden in vapour, and abrupt against it the box that covers the statue of Charles II in Roman armour, protecting him from bombs. To my left was the wreckage from a bomb explosion upon a wing of the hospital some weeks ago : a neat piece bitten out of Wren's building from top to bottom. This explosion had shaken the fabric of the long panelled chapel, for which James II gave the plate and furnishings. The Ricci painting of the Ascension in the apse of the chapel had been cracked and scratched : its yellow and brown surface is now chipped white by fragments of flying glass. Since the standards that used to hang all round the walls have been moved to safety, the chapel looks colourless and bare : only the plum-red cushions of the Governor's padded pew (beneath a group of oaken fluted columns that remind us of the lost treasures of St Lawrence Jewry) relieve the oak and plaster vacancy.

Before abandoning the sad search for Wren damage we must go to Greenwich. Here the destruction of the dome of the old observatory, designed by Wren in 1675, is the most noticeable example of bomb devastation. The Observatory, of universal fame as the source of Greenwich Mean Time, stands up on the crest of the hill behind Inigo Jones' Queen's House, with Spanish chestnut trees in lines, all that remains of Lenôtre's ambitious garden. The Observatory is interesting for many reasons, but particularly, I think, because it stresses the serious and progressive side of Restoration life. One tends to think of Charles II's court as all Lely and Grammont, all artifice and dissipation. We forget the scholarly and splendid contribution to world knowledge made under royal and aristocratic patronage at this time. With the closing years of William III's reign we are over the frontier of a new epoch, and approaching the great period of colonial warfare and the founding of the Empire. We can hear the hollow ringing of a thousand horses' shoes upon the Flemish turf, we can smell the powder in the air. There are new names upon everyone's lips : Oudenarde and Malplaquet, Ramillies and Blenheim. For the first time Churchill is a word of national significance. Yet England is already in the vanguard of those countries that cultivate the Arts of Peace. We see in Wren's London achievement—fifty-two churches, a cathedral, two palaces, a royal hospital, and many other buildings—that it is in the most constructive and least war-like of the arts that we excelled. Painting, Literature, and even Music can be made to serve political ends. Architecture such as that of Sir Christopher Wren demands as a pre-requisite to its existence certainty, safety, and immunity from attack.

*The Grounds of Chiswick House*

*Smith Square, Westminster*

# III

# THE ATTACK ON HANOVERIAN LONDON

*Aristocratic Rule in Eighteenth Century—Town Houses of the Nobility—Barbone and Wren—George I and Wren—Gibbs—Church of St Martin-in-the-Fields Injured—Early Georgian Court—Georgian Streets a Legacy—Doctor Johnson's House Burned—Hogarth's House at Chiswick Wrecked—Georgian London—Street Life—The Docks—The New Squares—Air-raid Damage to Georgian London—Generalisations on Destruction—Great Cumberland Place Worst Section—Regency London—Stucco versus High Explosive—The Regent's Park Terraces and Nash—Damage to the Terraces—Victorian London can no Longer be Ignored—Mammoth Buildings—Museum Land—Tesseræ and Terra-cotta—Damage to Victorian London too Widespread for Details—Romanesque Ruins—Paternoster Row—Langham Hotel—Damage to Museums—Gothic Revival Churches Gutted—Were the Victorians Humble ?—Neo-Gothic Skyline—the Frontispiece—The Attack on London's Past a Failure.*

IN the eighteenth century the English aristocracy was powerful and ostentatious. Owners of great country seats continued the traditions of the Tudor and Stuart nobility, building magnificent London houses, palaces with which we connect the names of Kent, Ripley, and the brothers Adam. We also connect these architects with the stately terraces and squares into which London, like L'Enfant's Washington or any other big city of this century, was being gradually patterned out. The terraces and squares remain to-day, some in name and situation only, but the majority with their Georgian housefronts undisturbed by twentieth-century progress. It is these placid and dignified streets that are now being pitted with German bombs. The great aristocratic houses, on the other hand, had disappeared long before this war—Chesterfield House, Devonshire House, Lansdowne House, Norfolk House, and the rest, their demolition an indirect result of working democracy. Their predecessors in elegance and grandeur, the Elizabethan mansions on the Thames bank, had also gone at the bidding of the speculative builder. In this case it was the famous Doctor Nicholas Barbone, who began by covering the site of old Essex House with alleys and pot-houses, and whose extended activities all over Charles II's London make him as memorable a figure as Sir Christopher Wren. It was upon and against the city of Wren and Barbone that Georgian London took its graceful shape.

It is, of course, imprecise to draw any distinction between the London of Wren and that of George I. In so far as that alien king can be said to have had a London at all, it was Wren's London. Wren died only four years before George I, and subsequent architecture continued to be deeply influenced by his theories and example. Wren's personal dominance depended, however, on the Stuart dynasty. With the Hanoverian entrance his enemies prevailed over him, and he was dismissed in 1718, a man of eighty, from his position as Surveyor-General. He retired to Hampton Court and died in 1723 of a chill caught on the journey between his house there and his house in London. Hawksmoor, his assistant and pupil, died in 1736. Georgian London was left with two major architectural figures: James Gibbs and William Kent. It was Gibbs who built St Peter Vere Street, St Mary-le-Strand, and St Martin-in-the-Fields.

St Martin-in-the-Fields is a large and very well-known church, owing its important position to the laying-out in 1829 of Trafalgar Square. The square covers ground once occupied by the royal mews of Whitehall Palace, and a warren of tiny streets known as the Bermudas. The old church of St Martin had become too small for its congregation, and in 1721 it was taken down. That St Martin's should prove inadequate for its parish would have struck Elizabethans as a conundrum: for many generations it had stood almost empty each Sunday, literally in the midst of uninhabited fields. With the Stuart thrust westwards the parish became populous and was carved up: St Paul's, Covent Garden, was cut out of it, and St James's, Piccadilly, and St Anne's, Soho. By Bishop Burnet's day St

94

Martin's was the largest cure in England : the removal of three parishes from it had not sufficiently reduced its size. So instead of making the parish any smaller it was decided to make the church bigger, and in 1726 Gibbs built a new one. During demolition work the vaults of St Martin's were found to be disgustingly crowded, and Aaron Hill wrote lines describing the sight :

> The pews pale squares in their whole lengthened row
> Gave way and opened a sad scene below !
> Beauty, youth, wealth, and power reduced to clay
> Larded with bones, yet moist, unsheltered lay :
> Remnants of eyeless skulls, with hollow stare,
> Mocked the proud looks which living charmers wear.

St Martin's vaults are now an air-raid shelter. The bomb damage to the church is not particularly severe.

Although a chapel was automatically erected in each new square, Georgian London was not especially religious. Sunday was suitably observed, church attendance was regular, Wesley and the Quakers had a certain following, and so later had the Countess of Huntington's connection : but the bag-wigged bishops are more typical of the age, as they sit calmly in their town houses in Cavendish or Grosvenor Square, fingering the gilded pages of a duodecimo *Horace*, or waiting to go to a debate in the House of Lords. The courts of the first two Georges, Germanic and guttural, set the tone for the aristocracy ; it was a gross tone, and it had nothing to do with the super-natural or with immortality. George I grunted politics all through the sermon, and the Maids of Honour of the Princess of Wales were screened off from the congregation in St James's Chapel Royal because they would giggle and ogle so. The coronation of George I, like his entry into London from Green-wich, had been heavy and solemn, but the reign which had opened with pomp continued as an anticlimax : the skirling bagpipes of the rebellion of fifteen, the public quarrels of George I and his heir (when on one occasion the Prince and Princess of Wales, ejected from St James's Palace, withdrew to hold a separate court at Leicester House), the South Sea Bubble, the long absences of King George in beloved Hanover.

Yet at first there is a kind of bloom upon the new reign. There is music on the Thames, trumpets and cymbals over the river as the Prince of Wales' barge glides back to London from the masques at Hampton Court. There is genius such as Pope's, talent like that of the architect Lord Burlington. It is an era of apparent civilisation but of great coarseness. Caroline, though able and intelligent, was hardly more refined than the Duchess of Kendal and George I's other German mistresses. Lord Chesterfield, so very polished and so very ugly, wasting a lifetime's worldliness in his famous letters to a fool, is fundamentally coarse. Doctor Johnson, gloomy and immortal, was physically filthy : even Lord Hervey's lovely oval face and swift adder mind concealed great toughness, and so indeed did the gravity and good sense of Mrs Howard, the mistress of the Prince of Wales. What is left for us from this eddying pool of intrigue and alexandrines, from these lives whirled away in Zoffany rooms and beneath Kent porticoes ? Besides painting and poetry, creased letters, spiteful diaries, and political tracts we have inherited the London streets in which we live. Georgian London was an essential part of their legacy to posterity, a legacy which, injured in the current war, must be repaired and not replaced.

By a deplorable coincidence the houses of two eighteenth-century Englishmen whose names are reverenced across the civilised globe have been wrecked by bombing. Doctor Johnson's house in Gough Square was well known to American visitors, though Hogarth's summer villa at Chiswick, a little purple brick cottage behind a brick wall, was not. I think that few English people bothered to go to Hogarth's house : it stood, as its battered walls still stand, in a lane close to the main gateway of Lord Burlington's Palladian villa, Chiswick House. In Hogarth's lifetime his house was in the open country : though the Italian residence built by Lord Burlington in the 1730's, and surrounded by yew walks, cypresses, artificial water, stone sphinxes, and antique Roman emperors (all the paraphernalia of the Augustan dream world), was near enough to give sophistication to his environment. Hogarth first went to Chiswick in the autumn of 1749, and continued to go there each summer until his death in London in 1764. He lived

*Bloomsbury Scene*

*The Statue of Dr. Johnson at St. Clement Danes, his Parish Church; and (left) remains of the attic in his house in Gough Square, Fleet Street, where the Dictionary was compiled*

there very simply with his wife, his dogs, and his bullfinch: giving the village children an annual feast of mulberries from the gnarled tree in the garden, and attending every Sunday the village church. We can think of him there as he painted himself in the portrait in the Tate Gallery, with a turban about his head and his dog and palette at his side, a plump, genial man. He lies buried in Chiswick churchyard, beneath a stone bearing Garrick's epitaph:

> Farewell, great painter of mankind,
> Who reached the noblest point of art:
> Whose pictured morals charm the mind,
> And through the eye correct the heart.

The little summer villa has been smashed now, and stands like a broken toy behind its high brick wall.

Doctor Johnson's house in Gough Square, up an alley off Fleet Street, has been saved from complete destruction by fire-fighters. Repair would be possible here, for only the long attic room at the top of the house is seriously harmed. This room, which is now roofless and damp, was used by Johnson and his amanuenses during the composition of his Dictionary. While work on the Dictionary was in progress Johnson lived, says Boswell, partly in Holborn and partly in Gough Square: "He had an upper room fitted up like a counting house for the purpose, in which he gave to the copyists their several tasks." The words were some of them taken from other dictionaries, some of them supplied by himself. They were methodically set out on pieces of paper, with spaces between them for derivation, etymology, and meaning. It was all very neatly done, and Boswell, seeing reference books used in the process, noticed that Dr Johnson had marked them in very light pencil and then rubbed that out. When it was published the Dictionary created vast excitement: it was the first English dictionary (perhaps it remains the only one) which could be read with instruction and pleasure: but it did not help Johnson's financial position at all. Boswell once said to him: "I am sorry, sir, you did not get more from your Dictionary." He replied: "I am sorry too. But it was very well. The book-sellers are generous, liberal-minded men."

Is there any more truly vivid character in Georgian England than Dr Johnson ? One imagines him, and also somehow remembers him, in so many different ways : paying the copyists for his Dictionary when he himself had no money, contradicting Boswell, writing to Mrs Thrale on her re-marriage, laughing in Dundonald Castle till the ruins echoed, popping his head (and his little black wig) out of the door of his rooms in the Temple when knocked up late one night to go on a drinking bout. His statue outside St Clement Danes, the island church in the Strand where he used to go regularly, has remained resolute amidst bombs which have exploded round it. One wonders what trenchant attitude Samuel Johnson would have adopted to present circumstance : and one recollects how, after many years spent in terror of dying, he faced his end firmly and hopefully, making to his servant Barber (who had brought him a letter) one of his last and most characteristic remarks : " An odd thought strikes me," he said quietly; " we shall receive no letters in the grave."

*    *    *    *

Unlike medieval London the city of the Georges is very easy for us to reconstruct. It was the age of the conversation piece, and we all know what Georgian saloons and kitchens, street brawls and theatres looked like. For the brothel atmosphere of the eighteenth century we have only to turn to Hogarth : for tempered elegance to Zoffany and Devis. We are here, however, narrowly concerned with the century's contribution to architecture, and how that contribution has been spoiled by German bombs. The squalors of Defoe's London—link-boys running in the gutters, drabs squabbling, carriage-wheels blundering through puddles, beggars huddled at corners, Newgate execution crowds, and the swarming pleasure grounds south of the river—do not, thank God, concern us. But it is important to notice the seamy aspect of the eighteenth-century city, to observe that under the Georgian kings London was sprawling eastwards down the river, and the foundations were being firmly laid for Victorian dockland and the slums. The London docks were built mainly at the very end of the eighteenth century to deal with the East and West

Indies' trade. The colonial wars with France and Spain had been chiefly fought out in, and fought out for, the American possessions. An almost fantastic importance was popularly attached to the green Caribbean harbours and the languid fields of waving cane. The prestige of the West Indies was due to the evident opulence of the merchants, whose houses began to flank the Whitechapel and Mile End roads, as the city spread east. Soon, however, shacks and tenements began to appear amongst the solid merchant mansions : and then brick-kilns, smoking sullenly all night, started to pollute the air. Rich houses were abandoned by their owners, divided up, and crammed with pauper families. In 1755 Bethnal Green was still open ground, but Stepney and its district, where Elizabethan herbalists had found penny royal, wild mallow, and scented orchis on the heath, and Pepys had walked between hedges woven with convolvulus, had become a built-up area. All the while that Kent and the Adams, and then Nash and Decimus Burton were decorating the aristocratic houses of north and western London, a disgraceful slum city was creeping east-wards over the meadows and downstream past the Isle of Dogs.

As early as 1715, the year of Queen Anne's death, plans were under way for the improvement of the land north of Tyburn Road, soon called Oxford Street. In 1717 Cavendish Square was laid out, and the whole of its north side taken by Lord Carnarvon, afterwards Duke of Chandos, for a huge house of which he only finished the two wings. In 1718 Hanover Square was set out and named in compliment to George I. A contemporary was impressed by the Tyburn Road development : " I passed an amazing scene of new foundations, not of houses only, but as I might say of new cities, new towns, new squares, and fine buildings, the like of which no city, no town, no place in the world can show." Grosvenor Square, begun under William and Mary, was now complete, and its houses taken on lease by such persons as Lord Chesterfield and the Duchess of Kendal. All about the new squares little streets, with chapels and mews, cropped up. As the century progressed building in West London (suspended about 1720 by the bursting of the South Sea Bubble and the slump that it occasioned) increased in speed : Portman Square was started in 1764, Harley Street,

Mansfield Street, and Portland Place in 1770, Great Cumberland Place in 1775, and so on.  From 1786 to 1792 the rate was accelerated under the guidance of the brothers Adam, whose influence on London streets is excellently shown in the south and east sides of Fitzroy Square.  Public buildings—Kent's Horse Guards, Ripley's Admiralty, the Treasury—had risen intermittently throughout the period.  The tide of taste in metropolitan development surged over into the nineteenth century, reaching its crest in the superb terraces and villas John Nash set about Regent's Park, in Regent Street, and the classical façade of Carlton House Terrace.  For a decade or two London architecture maintained this serene flood level : and then in the forties and fifties of the new century began to sink.

Almost every Georgian square in London has lost one or more houses through the air raids.  Like the first sight of the burned Wren churches, or the yellow rubble of Allhallows by the Tower, the heaps of dust and planking into which these houses have crumpled are very shocking.  Some of the finest of the houses seem like people who have given up hope : they have shrivelled into a handful of colourless lath and plaster.  Often there seems too little material in the wreckage to have made a house from, and the rubbish seems to bear less relationship to a building than the most shrivelled skeleton to a full-fleshed human being.  These familiar and symmetrical house fronts are revolting when they have been bombed.  The brickwork is leprous.  Where houses have been very badly damaged, we can stare up through the ceilings of splendid reception rooms, from floor to floor, where ghastly fragments of gilding still remain upon a cornice, or a Chippendale mirror is still screwed to a broken wall.  The worst piece of devastation, to my mind, is that at the corner of the crescent in Great Cumberland Place by Marble Arch.  These houses, intended in 1775 to form part of a circus that was never built, have been torn and blasted till they look like classical ruins.  This is the grimmest piece of bomb damage in West London.

Regency London—the Regent's Park terraces, Carlton House Terrace, the church of All Souls in Langham Place, University of London Hall, Belgravia—has suffered with the rest of the city and the centuries.  John Nash, who condemned

*Damage to Georgian London: the wrecked Crescent in Great Cumberland Place*

*A House in Kensington*

*The Effects of Fire in the Galleries of the Natural History Museum: the burned Herbarium, and scorched remains of the world-famous collection of dried plants*

*Cases and Exhibits in the*
*Natural History Museum,*
*South Kensington*

*A Broken Arc: Park Crescent to-day — and in the last century*

the jerry-building about Marylebone ("Marylebone temple builders" he called the architects), was himself considered unthorough by contemporary critics, combining "genius with carelessness . . . sometimes degenerating into littleness," and the perishable nature of his London improvements was ridiculed :

> Augustus at Rome was for building renown'd,
> For of marble he left what of brick he had found ;
> But is not our Nash, too, a very great master,
> He finds it all brick and leaves it all plaster.

Nash could not foresee that his stucco terraces would be asked to stand up to high explosive. Nor could the proprietor of Decimus Burton's Colosseum (a domed rotunda that dominated Regent's Park, and was thought by Rogers to be "finer than anything among the remains of architectural art in Italy"), imagine how ironical the artificial ruins with which he filled his grounds would one day seem. He would no more have believed that within a century Regent's Park would have real ruins instead of make-believe ones, than that the movies would supersede his London panorama, hall of mirrors, gothic aviary, and stalactite caves as places of popular amusement.

Under the influence of George IV England achieved a civic architecture unsurpassed for grace and beauty. As Prince Regent, George had rebuilt Carlton House to the designs of Henry Holland : and in 1812 he commissioned Nash to lay out Regent's Park. The park, originally known as Marylebone Fields, was planned to contain a palace for the Prince, villas for the rich, an artificial lake with a bridge and islands, the whole enclosed by a solemn series of classical terraces, with triumphal archways and entrance gates. This paradise was linked with Carlton House by Regent Street, running from St James's to Portland Place, and crossing Oxford Circus on its way. At the north end of this street All Souls, Langham Place, with its very elegant spire, appeared as through a vista : and beyond Portland Place a circus (of which Park Crescent was the only portion built) was to be cut in half by New Road. A great deal of this ambitious scheme was carried out : but Nash's Regent Street has been long since destroyed and replaced by the commonplace modern thoroughfare. The Regent's Park terraces had survived. People well acquainted with London will be bored by a description of the Nash terraces: to write of them is irresistible. These terraces are undoubtedly the most romantic pieces of architecture in all London: their stucco façades, their commanding unity, their triumphal arches, Corinthian or Ionic, their amplitude, solemnity and grandeur, their cool elegance in summer, the sun shining on their door-steps and the feathery trees giving them shade. Most wonderful of all, I used to think, was the sight of them on a winter's night, with the moonbeams glistening on the stucco, and powdered snow lying lightly on the ground. This magic and spacious series of terraces—fluted columns, Corinthian archways, and pavilions—could not, one felt, really be London. They seemed like imperial Leningrad, they seemed everything that is most nostalgic, romanticised, and remote from realities, cloudy creations of the mind as they glimmered in the frosty midnight and the silence. Here was a part of London that even air raids could not touch.

One's first doubts about the terraces' immunity, however, came with the tunnelling of Regent's Park for air-raid shelters. One glanced shyly but apprehensively at the raw brown mole-heaps on the green grass. The terraces themselves seemed consciously aloof from this subterranean activity. And then came the bombs. A night walk past the Nash terraces in 1941 convinced one of the futility of wishful thinking. The stucco is as white as ever in the moonlight, the trees as feathery; but at York Terrace a house has been blown in half, Clarence Terrace is gutted and empty (the shutters wrenched from their hinges, the doors battered in): the cupolas of Sussex Place have trembled at the bombs: Chester Terrace has lost its windows, and begins to show the peeling dankness of structural decay. All along the white façades the window-frames gape jagged and black in the light of the February moon.

Up to the moment of the air raids we never had to analyse our feelings towards Victorian London, the city of Cruikshank and Dickens, of gas lamps and jubilees. We did not try to define our attitude towards the architecture of the Langham Hotel; we accepted it as a natural part of the Portland Place landscape. In spite of Edwardian and neo-Georgian demolition, and the sudden appearance of places like Bush House, we accepted what we had been left by the nineteenth century without comment. Occasionally one might come upon some piece of Victoriana—a doorway in Lower Thames Street, perhaps, or a Gothic annexe to a mansion in Kensington Palace Gardens—that seemed interesting or startling : but on the whole we took over the Victorian city just as the Jacobeans took over that of the Renaissance. And by the end of the nineteenth century London was in the truest sense a Victorian city. Mammoth buildings—hotels, museums, offices, and churches—had begun, in the fifties and sixties, to elbow their way in amongst the geometric patterns of Georgian London, and to darken the narrow streets of the City left by Wren and the Commissioners. At first they were isolated marvels of tile and terra-cotta, but very soon they made it evident that they had come to stay : they supplanted the houses of older London, and to-day we do not often find a Victorian structure standing alone amongst Georgian ones. The position of the Austin Friars Church, or of that called St Benets, Paul's Wharf, are indicative of the state of affairs. Instead of old London Bridge we have Tower Bridge with its mechanical contrivances ; instead of river palaces we have the Embankment, that very uncompromising promenade ; instead of Kensington village we have a solemn phalanx of museums " Italian in general effect." The museum buildings at South Kensington are wholly characteristic of their epoch. The iron structure of the first museum was erected in 1856, and called by contemporary wits " the boilers." One of the novelties of the new museumland by the Cromwell and Exhibition Roads was the liberal use of coloured materials : red bricks of two tints, terra-cottas of crimson and " a pale but not harshly white hue," tile tesseræ " of chocolate and warm grey," majolica with a white ground relieved by yellow and blue. Terra-cotta was indeed a favourite substance in the sixties. The decorations of the Albert Hall (the first stone of which was laid by the queen in the spring of 1867) were made of it, so were the shafts of the chimney-stacks of the Charing Cross Hotel (which also had " a very bold ornament in stamped zinc " along its roof-tops). It is sometimes a little difficult to realise that Victorian monumental architecture was intended to be not only impressive but gay.

The damage to Victorian London? This cannot be explicitly stated; it includes too much. The largest nineteenth-century area destroyed was that part of the city burned at the end of 1940, publishers' houses, drapers' shops, office buildings, restaurants: the Romanesque style of the sixties (exemplified in Paternoster Row by Longmans and the Religious Tract Society) turned into classical ruins. The Langham Hotel in Portland Place, considered "a sumptuous pile" when erected by Giles and Murray in the sixties, has been so badly shattered that its tiered window frames seemed at one moment to emulate a Piranesi. All through the streets of London that genial amalgam of styles that constitutes the basic eccentricity of Victorian architectural taste has been scarred and jolted by bombs. From the Holbeinesque houses of Pont Street and the Cadogans right away to the trim villas of St John's Wood, from Blackheath to Pimlico and Kensington, the damage extends. Victorian builders knew their job: and the solidity with which their houses have stood up to high explosive contrasts sadly with the powdered brick and plaster of Georgian streets. The museums in Kensington have been slightly disturbed: the Herbarium of the Natural History Museum, known to botanists the world over, has been gutted, and blast has played curious pranks with some of the exhibits in other parts of this building. The gaunt Gothic churches of the suburbs have had casualties in their ranks. Their outraged walls seem pathetic, and not, like the medieval and Stuart church ruins, deeply tragic.

The respectful affection which we feel for Victorian London is something very deeply ingrained in ourselves. In the twenty years between two wars we have been laughing at the Victorians —at their tastelessness, their prudery, their Gothic, their gas-jets, and their railway stations. The laughter has begun to ring a trifle hollow: and we glance back at them with a new respect. What admirable generations, with all their self-importance and their confidence, grew up during that long beneficent reign! A serious examination of the London buildings they have left us reveals qualities that we do not at first suspect: there seems, we feel, to have been a kind of humility about the

*The House of Lords*

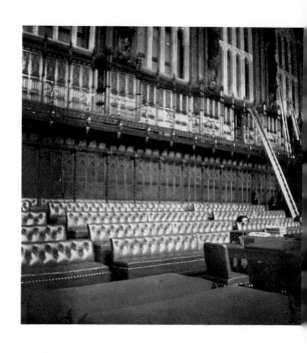

The broken windows of the House of Lords are boarded

The Abbey, and Statue of Richard Cœur de Lion (with sword bent by blast), seen through the twisted windows of Lord Halifax's room in the House of Lords

creators of these mammoth structures, and a foggy romanticism, and an obtuseness such as we sometimes see in the very rich. In architecture the Victorians realised, almost modestly, what they could not do. For each big building they erected they turned their eyes to the past, to the Gothic world, or to the Renaissance. Their aims were not, however, wholly imitative : for they felt themselves equipped to produce something better than the past—their own interpretation of it. The Gothic roof they put upon the Guildhall was probably considered superior to that which had been burned in the Great Fire. This same blindness prevented them from seeing how their romanticism had failed : and that the skyline of the Law Courts, the crockets of the St Pancras Hotel, the inside of the Public Records Office, and the " spire-capped " roofing of the Cannon Street Station were not only unsuccessful but thoroughly absurd.

The photograph which has been placed as frontispiece to this book shows us St Paul's Cathedral through the shattered doorway of a Victorian shop-front. Another elsewhere in the volume gives a view of Westminster Abbey through the twisted Gothic windows of a room in Barry's House of Lords.

These two illustrations epitomise the damage done to London's architecture. It is mainly buildings of small æsthetic merit (and often of no historical interest) that have been bombed. We must not underrate our losses ; yet a walk through any section of the city shows how much remains. The number of Wren's churches standing is far greater than that of those that have been burned. The brunt of the *Blitzkrieg* has been borne by houses and streets that are not, from the historical angle, of great significance. It is a narrow, perhaps even an inhuman, viewpoint—but seen from it the bombers' attack upon our London past has failed.

# INDEX

(The numerals in italics refer to the *page numbers* of illustrations)

Adam, the brothers, 93, 101
Albert Hall, 109
All Souls, Langham Place, 107
Allhallows Barking, 4, *8*, 10-17, 47, 102
Anne Boleyn, Queen, 18, 22
Anne, Queen, 66, 71, 84, 87
Austin Friars, Church of, 4, 5, 7, 10, 45, 109

Baker, Sir Richard, 55
Barbone, Dr Nicholas, 34
Barking, Abbey of, 15
Baxter, Richard, 70
Beauchamp, Sir John, 61
Billingsgate Market, 77
Blanche of Lancaster, 9
Bloomsbury Square, *97*
Bohun, Henry de, 4
Boswell, William, 99-100
Buckingham, third Duke of, 5
Burlington, Earl of, 96
Burton, Decimus, 101, 107

Carmelites, 4
Caroline, Queen, 88, 96
Catherine Howard, Queen, 18, 22
Cavendish Square, 101
Chamberlain, Neville, 41
Charing Cross, 82, 109
Charles I, statue of, 82
Charles II, 47, 77
Charterhouse, the, 28, 29
Cheapside, 62
Chelsea Hospital, 82, 89
Chesterfield House, 93
Chesterfield, Lord, 96, 101
Chichele, Archbishop, 34
Chiswick House, *91*, 96
Christ Church, Newgate, 45, *63*, *64*, 65, 69-71
City, the night of 30th December, *14*
Condell, Henry, 72
Cowper, William, 24
Culpeper, Thomas, 22
Cromwell, Thomas, 18
Crutched Friars, 4

Defoe, Daniel, 100
Dereham, Francis, 22

Devonshire House, 93
Digby, Sir Kenelm, 70
Digby, Lady, 70
Dissolution of the monasteries, 3, 5, 69
Dorchester, Catherine Sedley, Countess of, 84, 87
Dorset, Charles Sackville, sixth Earl of, 87
Dorset, Thomas Sackville, first Earl of, 55
Dugdale, Sir Miles, 101
*Dutch Church.* See Austin Friars

Edward II, 16, 36
Edward IV, 5, 61
Edward VI, 5
Elizabeth, Queen, 42
Evelyn, John, 77, 83

Fire, the Great, 3, 6, 10, *12-13*, 23, 70, 75, *81*
Fire-fighters: ancient and modern, *1*
Fisher, Bishop John, 17
Flodden, battle of, 18
Foxe, John, 24, 27
Frobisher, Sir Martin, 24, 27

George I, 94, 95, 101
Gibbs, James, 94
Gloucester, Eleanor, Duchess of, 22
Goldsmith, 37
Great Cumberland Place, 102, *103*
Greenwich Observatory, 89
Grey, Lady Jane, 21, 22
Grosvenor Square, 101
Guildhall, the, 10, *19*, 22-24, 43, *57*, 113

Hanover Square, 101
Harley Street, 101
Hatton, Sir Christopher, tomb of, 9
Heming, William, 71
Henrietta Maria, Queen, 6, 30, 83
Henry III, 30, 35, 41, 65
Henry IV, 36, 39
Henry V, 39, 40
Henry VI, 15
*Henry VI*, Shakespeare's, 77
Hill, Aaron, 95
Hogarth, William, 96, 99

Holborn, 17
Hollar, Wenceslas, 51

Inner Temple, the, 17

James II, 48, 87, 89
Jeffreys, Judge, 71
Jermyn, Henry, Earl of St Albans, 83
Jermyn Street, 83
Jewel House, the, 21
John of Gaunt, 9
Johnson, Dr Samuel, 96, 100
Johnson, Dr Samuel, house in Gough
   Square, *98*
Johnson, Dr Samuel, statue at St Clement
   Danes, *98*
Jones, Inigo, 72
Jonson, Ben, 28, 70

Kendal, Duchess of, 101
Kensington, house in, *103*
Kensington Palace, 82, 88
Kensington Palace Gardens, 109
Kent, Earl of, 4
Kent, William, 93, 94, 101
Knights Templar, 16, 17, 29, 30

Laing, Archbishop, 35
Lambeth Palace, 34, 45
Laud, 17, 35
Layer Marney, 35
Layfield, 17
Langham Hotel, 108, 109
Lansdowne House, 93
London Bridge, 6, 109
London Wall, 6
Lords, the House of, *111*, *112*

Manningham, John, 33
Manny, Sir John, 29
Marlborough, Duke of, 87
Mary I, 10, 22
Mary II, 66, 88
Middle Temple, *31*, *37*
Middle Temple Hall, 17, 30-33, *32*
Milton, John, 24, *25*
More, Sir Thomas, 18, 65

Nash, John, 101, 102
Natural History Museum, *104*, *105*, 110
Nelson, Monument to Lord, *19*, 23
Norfolk, John, second Duke of, 6
Norfolk, Thomas, third Duke of, 21, 22

Palace Yard, *38*
Paris, 16
Park Crescent, Portland Place, *103*, *106*
Pepys, Samuel, 10, 23, 47
Pepys, Mrs Samuel, 51
Philippe le Beau, 16
Pierrepoint, Lady Grace, 66, 87
Plague, the Great, 75
Poitiers, 16
Pole, Cardinal, 18
Pope, Alexander, 62, 96
Popish Plot, the, 77
Portland Place, 101
Portman Square, 101

Regent's Park, 102, 108
Ricci, Sebastian, 89
Richard I, 17, 30
Richard I, statue of, 36, *112*
Richard II, 35, 36
Richardson, Samuel, 56
Richmond House, 93
Richmond, Mary, Duchess of, 27
Ripley, Thomas, 93
Rochford, Viscountess, 18
Roubiliac, Louis François, 40
Rysbrack, 40

St Alban, Wood Street, 65, 72-76, *79*, *80*
St Andrew-by-the-Wardrobe, *49*, *50*, 51, 56,
   61
St Andrew Undershaft, *26*
St Anne and St Agnes, 46, 65, *68*, 72, *73*
St Anne's, Soho, 66, 84, *86*, 88
St Antholin, Budge Row, 52, 56
St Augustine with St Faith, 65
St Bartholomew the Great, 4, 48
St Benet Fink, 52
St Benet Gracechurch, 52
St Benet, Paul's Wharf, 109
St Benet Sherehog, 51
St Bride, Fleet Street, *43*, *44*, 52-56, 75
St Clement Danes, *98*, 100
St Dionis Backchurch, 52
St Giles, Cripplegate, *20*, 24, *25*, 27, 51
St Helen, Bishopsgate, 4, 51
St James, Garlickhythe, 69
St James's, Piccadilly, 55, 82, 83-88, *85*
St John Zachary, 72
St Lawrence Jewry, 45, *57*, *58*, *59*, *60*, 65-69,
   83
St Lawrence Poultney, 69
St Magnus, London Bridge, 76
St Margaret Pattens, *26*, 51

St Margarets Westminster, *38*
St Martin-in-the-Fields, 94
St Martin Pomeroy, 52
St Mary Abchurch, 45, 76
St Mary, Aldermanbury, 65, *67*, 71-72
St Mary Aldermary, 51
St Mary-at-Hill, 76
St Mary-le-Bow, 51, *53*, 56-62
St Mary-le-Strand, 94
St Mary Mounthaw, 52
St Mary Vere Street, 94
St Michael Paternoster Royal, 51
St Mildred, Bread Street, 28
St Mildred Poultney, 52
St Nicholas Acon, 52
St Nicholas Cole Abbey, 51
St Nicholas Flee Shambles, 69
St Olave, Hart Street, 28, 51
St Paul's Cathedral, Western Campanile,
   *Frontispiece*, 2, *11*, *74*, 78-82
St Paul's, Old, 4, 9, 81
St Peter ad Vincula, 51
St Peter at Paul's Wharf, 52
St Peter, Cornhill, 45
St Stephen, Coleman Street, 65, 72-76
St Stephen, Walbrook, 51
St Vedast Foster, 51, *54*, 69
Seymour of Sudeley, Lord, 21
Shakespeare, William, 33, 71
Shrewsbury, Countess of, 18
Sissinghurst Castle, 35
Smith Square, *92*
Smithfield, 18
Speed, John, 24
Spenser, Edmund, 29
Stow, John, 1, *26*, 27, 28, 42, 62
Suffolk, Henry Grey, Duke of, 21, 22

Surrey, Henry Howard, Earl of, 17
Surrey, Richard Fitzalan, Earl of, 5

Temple, the, 29-33, *37*
Thornhill, Sir James, *59*, 65, 76
Tijou, ironwork in St Paul's, *74*
Tillotson, Archbishop, 66
Tower Hill, 18
Tower of London, the, 6, 9, 21
Tower Street, 10
*Twelfth Night*, Shakespeare's, 33, 34
Tyburn Tree, 18

Uncumber, Rood of St, 52

Victoria, Queen, 88, 89

Wellington, monument to Duke of, 23
Westminster Abbey, 4, 6, 39, 40-41, 113
Westminster Hall, 35, 36, *38*, 39
Whittington, Richard, 23, 24
Wilkinson's *Londina Illustrata*, *12-13*, 78
William III, 66, 77, 88
Winchester, William Paulet, first Marquess
   of, 5, 21
Winchester, third Marquess of, 5
Winter, Sir William, 17
Worde, Wynkyn de, 55
Wren's Pew in St Margaret Pattens, *26*
Wyatt, Sir Thomas, 21

Yeveley, Henry de, 35

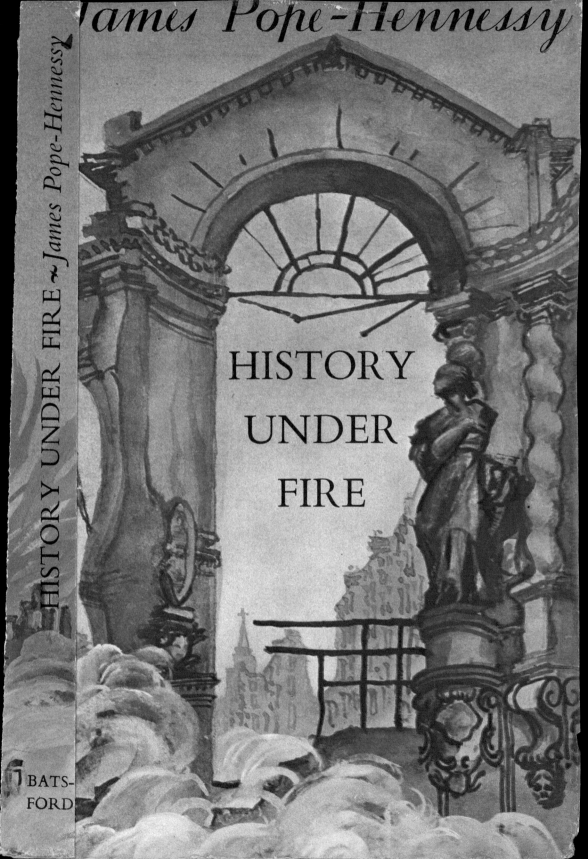